WEAPON

THE M16

GORDON L. ROTTMAN

Series Editor Martin Pegler

First published in Great Britain in 2011 by Osprey Publishing, Midland House, West Way, Botley, Oxford, OX2 0PH, UK 44-02 23rd Street, Suite 219, Long Island City, NY 11101, USA

E-mail: info@ospreypublishing.com

Osprey Publishing is part of the Osprey Group

A CIP catalog record for this book is available from the British Library

Print ISBN: 978 1 84908 690 5

PDF ebook ISBN: 978 1 84908 691 2

ePub ebook ISBN: 978 1 84908 891 6

Page layout by Mark Holt

Battlescene artwork by Johnny Shumate

Cutaway by Alan Gilliland

Index by Marie Pierre-Evans

Typeset in Sabon and Univers

Originated by Blenheim Colour

Printed in China through Worldprint

11 12 13 14 15   10 9 8 7 6 5 4 3 2 1

Osprey Publishing is supporting the Woodland Trust, the UK's leading woodland conservation charity, by funding the dedication of trees.

Acknowledgments

The author is indebted to Trey Moore (of Moore Militaria) and David Trantham. He is grateful, too, to Frederick Adolphus of the Ft Polk Museum, Louisiana; and to Jeff Hunt and Jean and Bob Gates of the Texas Military Forces Museum, Austin.

Front cover imges are courtesy of iStock and the US Department of Defense.

Editor's note

Metric cartridge designations (e.g. 7.62×54mm) identify first the bullet caliber (in millimeters) and second the case length (in millimeters).

Conversions

The measurements in this book are provided in US customary units, except for technical measurements that are specified in metric and the majority of ranges. For exact conversion between US customary and metric measurements note:

1 yard = 0.9144 meters
1 foot = 0.3048 meters
1 inch = 25.4 millimeters
1 pound = 0.4536 kilograms
1 grain = 64.79891 milligrams
1 ounce = 28.3495 grams
1 gallon = 3.7854 liters
1 quart = 0.94635 liters

List of abbreviations

ACOG:	Advanced Combat Optical Gunsight (pronounced "a-cog")
ARVN:	Army of the Republic of Vietnam (pronounced "ar-vin")
BAR:	Browning Automatic Rifle (M1918A2) (pronounced "B-A-R")
CAR-15:	Colt Automatic Rifle (pronounced "car-fifteen")
FN:	*Fabrique Nationale* (National Fabrication)
fps:	feet per second
GLAD:	Grenade Launcher Attachment Development (M203)
H&K:	Heckler and Koch
IMR:	Improved Military Rifle (powder)
KAC:	Knight Armament Corporation
LSA:	Lubricant, Small Arms
MACV:	Military Assistance Command, Vietnam (pronounced "mac-vee")
MIL-STD:	Military Standard (official specifications for equipment)
m/s:	meters per second
MWS:	Modular Weapon System (tactical rails add-on)
RAS:	Rail Adapter System (tactical rails)
RAW:	Rifleman's Assault Weapon
rpm:	rounds per minute
SAC:	Strategic Air Command
SAW:	Squad Automatic Weapon (M249 light machine gun) (pronounced "saw")
SEAL:	Sea–Air–Land (Naval Special Warfare Force)
SMG:	submachine gun
SOPMOD:	Special Operations Peculiar Modification kit (for M4A1 carbine)
SPIW:	Special Purpose Individual Weapon
SPR:	Special Purpose Rifle
STANAG:	NATO Standardization Agreement (pronounced "sta-nag")

www.ospreypublishing.com

CONTENTS

INTRODUCTION

In 1958 a compact, uniquely designed rifle was introduced to the world as the ArmaLite .223cal AR-15. This revolutionary weapon was made of lightweight materials – special aluminum and plastics – not previously used in weapons except on a limited experimental basis. Its design, too, was new, although features were borrowed from earlier weapons. The XM16E1 was adopted in 1962 for special purpose use by Army special forces, airborne, and airmobile troops as well as for the Air Force's Security Police guarding nuclear weapons. In 1965 the M16 began to be issued to other Army and Marine units in Vietnam to provide a lighter and easier-to-use weapon than the heavy 7.62mm M14 rifle. Its use spread, and through the early 1970s it was issued throughout the Army and Marine Corps to be used worldwide. A number of variants, including submachine-gun and carbine versions, were also fielded. The M16 and its variants have been used by almost 70 countries, either as a standard shoulder arm, to supplement regular arms, or as special purpose weapons. The M16's 5.56×45mm cartridge, too, was revolutionary, though with flaws, and was adopted by NATO in 1980. It is now among the most-used combat cartridges in the world. Over 8,000,000 M16s and variants have been built and production continues.

The M16 "black rifle" has arguably been the most controversial rifle ever introduced in any army, with a long history of design defects, ruggedness issues, cleaning difficulties, reliability problems in harsh conditions, and poor ammunition performance. Searches are under way to find a replacement weapon and have been for many years. While it is riddled with problems, potential replacements to date have not demonstrated sufficient benefits to warrant the excessive cost of replacement; it is currently widely used and will remain in production for some time. It can be expected to stay in use for at least another two decades even if a replacement is adopted in the coming years. Taking into account its modern variants, the M16 rifle family is the longest-serving rifle in the US armed forces, 49 years at the time of writing.

OPPOSITE
A Navy SEAL emerges from a cloud of green smoke during a 1994 small-boat training exercise. He is armed with an M4A1 carbine, the full-automatic version of the M4, used by special operations forces. The M4 is instead capable of three-round bursts. (Leif Skoogfors/Corbis)

DEVELOPMENT
Enter the "black rifle"

In the late 1950s and early 1960s the status of US military shoulder arms was in a state of flux. The .30cal M1 Garand rifle, which had seen the US Army and Marines through World War II and the Korean War, was still in use and would arm some support units well into the 1960s and the National Guard and Reserve into the 1970s.

The 7.62mm M14 rifle was adopted in 1957, but series production and issue did not begin until 1959. The M14, while an effective weapon, was really not much of an improvement over the Garand. The M14 was about 2in longer, 0.8lb lighter, had a 20-round detachable magazine as opposed to the M1's eight-round clip, and used a different gas system. Technically the M14 was selective fire – semi- and full-automatic – but standard rifles had a selector lock preventing full-automatic fire. The M14 was intended to replace the M1 rifle, M2 carbine, M1918A2 Browning Automatic Rifle (or BAR), and M3A1 submachine gun ("grease gun"). The automatic rifle version of the M14, the M15 with a heavier barrel, bipod, shoulder rest, and selective fire, was standardized, but never went into production owing to a cost-cutting measure. Instead, standard light-barrel M14s with M2 bipods and the selector lock removed would replace the BAR. However, this proved to be totally inadequate, as did the later "improved" M14A1 automatic rifle.[1] Nor did the M14 replace the .45cal grease gun. Submachine guns (Thompsons and grease guns) had been largely replaced by the selective-fire M2 carbine at the end of World War II. However, grease guns remained in use as on-board equipment for tanks

---

[1] Development of the M14E2 began in 1963. It was first issued in 1965 and redesignated the M14A1 in 1966. It had a special straight-line stock, pistol grip, forearm handgrip, and muzzle compensator to improve accuracy, but offered little improvement

into the 1990s when they were finally replaced by the M4 carbine, a variant of the M16A2.

Besides M1 rifles, M2 carbines and BARs also remained in use by National Guard and Reserve units into the 1970s. Carbines were also used by Army Special Forces and US Air Force Security Police. The latter guarded Strategic Air Command (SAC) nuclear weapons and both organizations considered the aging carbines to be short-ranged and underpowered. The M2 carbine did have one benefit for the SAC guards; it would not do much damage to parked aircraft. It fired the small .30 Carbine round, barely more than a pistol cartridge, very different from the .30-06 Springfield round used in the M1 rifle, BAR, and Browning machine guns.

Both Army Special Forces and the Air Force were looking for a new lightweight weapon. The Air Force was the only service not to adopt the M14. One weapon of interest was offered by a new arms company, the ArmaLite Corporation, whose AR-15 rifle fired an unusual little .223cal round, much smaller than most period military cartridges, which were in the .30cal (7.62mm) range. The story of the eventual procurement and standardization of the M16 was steeped in inter-service conflict, rivalries, politics, gamesmanship, and simple ineptitude. This study focuses on the US military models: the M16, XM16E1, XM177E1, XM177E2, M16A1, M16A2, M16A3, M16A4, M4, M4A1, and Mk 12. The scores of civilian, law-enforcement, foreign derivatives, and developmental models, and the many commercially made accessories, are not addressed here.

In October 1954 the ArmaLite Division of the Fairchild Engine and Airplane Corporation was created with George Sullivan as president, Charles Dorchester as plant manager, and Eugene Stoner as chief engineer. Throughout 1956 Stoner filed patent applications for design features that would be incorporated into the AR-10 and AR-15. A .22cal version of the T48 (FN) rifle, a competitor of the T44 (the M14), was tested, but this was counterproductive as the weapon was just as heavy as the 7.62mm version.

Stoner was mainly interested in developing a 7.62mm rifle, namely the AR-10, but there were calls for a .22cal selective-fire rifle with a weight of

A drill sergeant and marksmanship committee instructor coach an infantry trainee (infantry trainees wore camouflage covers, basic trainees did not) in firing an XM16E1 rifle in full-automatic fire. It is fitted with an XM3 cloth-pin bipod. This type of bipod clipped on and was non-folding. (Ft Polk Museum)

7

The 5.56mm AR-15 rifle as issued to ARVN troops and US advisors in 1963. Note the lack of "fencing," the rounded ridge around the magazine release button (above the forward end of the trigger guard), the lack of forward assist device (FAD), the "waffle-pattern" 20-round magazine, and the prong-type flash suppressor. (Darkhelmet322)

less than 6lb and a 20-round magazine. It was to have at least the wounding capability of the .30cal carbine. The first specification called for a 300-yard effective range; this was raised to 400 yards and then 500 yards. The .222cal AR-15 was developed when Stoner, assisted by Robert Fremont and Jim Sullivan, scaled down the AR-10. The design would require a great deal of tweaking over the coming years. The president of Fairchild accompanied the SAC commander on an African hunting safari in 1957 and there is little doubt that a pitch was made for the AR-15.

In May 1957 Stoner demonstrated the AR-15 at the Infantry School, Ft Benning, Georgia. This was just days after the Army formally adopted the M14. Ten AR-15 rifles in .222 Remington Special (the caliber that evolved into the .223 Remington, which in turn became the 5.56mm), were tested along with the .224 Winchester lightweight military rifle – which was of more conventional design with a wood stock, appearing as a cross between the M1 carbine and M14 rifle – for the Small Caliber High Velocity Rifle program. The Ordnance .22cal T48 rifle failed the tests. The AR-15 experienced 6.1 malfunctions per 1,000 rounds. The Infantry Board assessed that both the AR-15 and the Winchester were potential replacements for the M14 and, if fitted with a shoulder rest and a bipod, could replace the M15 automatic rifle. It was suggested that a soldier with a .223cal weapon could carry 650 rounds as opposed to an M14-armed soldier with 220 rounds. However, even then it was realized that the small-caliber round lacked the penetration of the 7.62mm. There were also problems with water retention in the small bore resulting in burst barrels as well as positional disclosing issues owing to muzzle flash. In August 1958 the Infantry Board found that further development was necessary for both weapons. Winchester, however, opted out of further trials.

Through early 1959 there was a great deal of debate on the future of the AR-15 with some urging further testing as a replacement for the M14 (which had not yet entered production), others recommending that testing cease, and still others recommending that it no longer be considered as a replacement for the 7.62mm, but as a special purpose weapon. On February 19, 1959, ArmaLite licensed the AR-10 and AR-15 to Colt Manufacturing Company of Hartford, Connecticut, a major management and financial mistake on ArmaLite's part. Colt paid ArmaLite US$75,000 plus a 4.5 percent royalty on production. Colt began marketing the rifles; it found little interest in the AR-10, but small numbers of AR-15s were ordered by Australia, Burma, India, Malaya, and Singapore. In May the

Eugene M. Stoner – father of the M16

Eugene Stoner was born in Gosport, Indiana, on November 22, 1922. His family soon moved to Long Beach, California, where he graduated from the Long Beach Polytechnical High School. In the Depression years there was no money for him to attend college for the engineering degree he desired. In 1939 his first job was installing aircraft armament for Vega Aircraft Company on Hudson bombers. Stoner served in the Marine Corps as an enlisted aviation ordnance technician working on large-caliber automatic weapons. He served from 1942 to 1945 in the Philippines, on Okinawa, and in North China.

In 1945, Stoner went to work for the Whittaker Corporation, an aircraft equipment firm, and worked his way up to design engineer regardless of his lack of an engineering degree. During this period he was independently working on small-arms designs. In 1954 he was hired as chief engineer for the new ArmaLite Division of the Fairchild Engine and Airplane Corporation in Hollywood, California. The new firm's concept was to design weapons using the latest technological advances in aircraft alloys and plastics. Stoner designed the AR-5 (.22 Hornet survival rifle for the Air Force), AR-7 (.22cal survival rifle), AR-9 and AR-17 (12-gauge semi-automatic shotguns), AR-11 (experimental .222cal semi-automatic rifle), and many others. Other than the AR-7 survival rifle, these were not commercially successful designs, but were noteworthy in their developmental advancement. Of course Stoner's most successful designs were the 7.62mm AR-10 combat rifle and 5.56mm AR-15 automatic rifle. He had less success with the later AR-18 assault rifle.

In 1959 the AR-15 was licensed to Colt Firearms leaving the AR-7 survival rifle, with limited sales, as the only weapon the company had in production. Stoner left ArmaLite and signed on with Colt as a consultant in 1961. The following year he began to work for Cadillac Gage and developed the 5.56mm Stoner 63 modular weapons system, capable of being configured into six weapons.

Although it saw combat testing in Vietnam, it was never adopted as the M16A1 was already undergoing wide distribution. Stoner had defeated his new design with an earlier one, the M16. Stoner later undertook developmental work for TRW on the 25mm M242 Bushmaster automatic cannon used on Bradley fighting vehicles. In 1971 Stoner co-founded ARES, Incorporated in Port Clinton, Ohio, where he designed the Ares machine gun and the Future Assault Rifle System. In 1977 Eugene Stoner was inducted into the US Army Ordnance Corps Hall of Fame. Leaving ARES in 1989, he went to work for Knight's Armament Corporation (KAC) in Titusville, Florida the following year. It was there that he developed the Stoner 96 weapon system and the .50cal SR-50 and 7.62mm SR-25 sniper rifles; the latter is still in use by the US armed forces as the Mk 11 Mod 0. That same year Stoner met his Russian counterpart, Mikhail Kalashnikov (1919–), designer of the notorious AK-47, a weapon usually on the other side of the front line facing the M16 and the most prodigiously produced assault rifle in the world. The meeting was arranged by Edward Ezell, small-arms curator of the Smithsonian Institution, and the two legendary weapons designers discussed and fired each other's weapon.

During his career Stoner amassed over 100 weapons-related patents, becoming one of America's most prolific arms designers. It is estimated that Stoner received approximately one dollar in royalties for each M16 produced. According to a colleague, Stoner was "the master of the obvious. When he came up with an idea you would ask yourself, 'Why didn't I think of that?'" Eugene Stoner died in Palm City, Florida, on April 24, 1997 and was survived by his second wife and four children. In 2002 the Marine Corps established the Stoner Award for Acquisition Excellence and Innovation to be awarded annually to Marine NCOs recognizing their professional excellence and/or innovation in pursuit of acquisition, fielding, and/or support of systems and equipment to the operating forces.

Combat Development Experimentation Center released a report stating that a 5–7-man squad with AR-15s could theoretically hit more targets than an 11-man squad armed with M14s.

In July 1960 the AR-15 was demonstrated and fired by Air Force General Curtis LeMay. He promised to recommend it as a replacement for the M2 carbine. Testing of ten rifles was conducted through the summer of 1960. Additional Army Ordnance testing was undertaken and the improved AR-15s suffered only 2.5 malfunctions out of 1,000 rounds. Colt made major efforts to market the AR-15 and receive some form of US armed forces adoption; this would allow foreign countries receiving US military aid to use US funding to purchase AR-15s. In November the Air Force was authorized

to conduct further trials. Testing showed that 43 percent of AR-15 firers scored Expert while only 22 percent of M14 firers achieved the same level. This was due to the AR-15's flatter trajectory and higher velocity.

Much of 1961 saw a battle fought between the Air Force and the Department of Defense and various government and Army agencies over LeMay's insistence upon the acquisition of 80,000 AR-15s. Arguments against it included the availability of the M2 carbine despite its age, recommendations for other rifles, Congressional reluctance to allocate funds for a new weapon after the expense of developing the M14, inconsistency with NATO standardization objectives, the introduction of a new caliber, and the need to stock an additional spare-parts inventory.

In August LeMay took a different approach. President Kennedy had directed that all the armed services expand their capabilities to conduct counterinsurgency warfare. For the Air Force this meant the Composite Air Strike Forces and Air Commandos (redesignated Special Operations in 1968), especially those deployed to Southeast Asia. In September the Department of Defense approved the Air Force's purchase of 8,500 AR-15s. LeMay's badgering of the Army was so insistent that President Kennedy warned him to back off. However, Military Assistance and Advisory Group, Vietnam (MAAG-V) recognized that the heavy M1 rifle and BAR were ill-suited for small-statured Army of the Republic of Vietnam (ARVN) troops and that M2 carbines, while light and compact, were inadequate for jungle warfare and could not stand up to the 7.62mm SKS carbine and AK-47 assault rifle. Small numbers of AR-15s were received for field testing by the ARVN. With favorable results, MAAG-V had their request for 1,000 AR-15s approved. LeMay was making little headway in gaining approval for additional AR-15s, even being personally rejected by Kennedy. At the end of 1961 Fairchild sold the exclusive license and patent rights of the AR-15 to Colt.

In January 1962 the Air Force standardized the AR-15 rifle as the M16, but further procurement was not in the budget. In May the

American Rifleman magazine published an article complaining of the AR-15's performance in cold weather, inaccuracy, and poor reliability, and recommending that the rifling twist should be changed from 1-in-14in to 1-in-12in (one turn in 12in of bore). That same month the Appropriations Committee challenged the Air Force to respond to the *American Rifleman* article as they had resubmitted the request for 80,000 AR-15s. Impressed with the Air Force's response, they granted the request. The Navy SEALs purchased 172 AR-15s for testing. In July reports from Vietnam stated the AR-15 was the best all-round weapon and should replace the M1 rifle, M2 carbine, BAR, and Thompson submachine gun in the ARVN. Indeed, the first combat use of the AR-15 was by the ARVN; it saw its second conflict in the Indonesia–Malaysia Confrontation on Borneo in 1963, where it was used by the Australian SAS.

Conflicting reports were released in September, criticizing or praising the AR-15. The main concern was that the M14 was already in production and being issued to units. Changing to a new rifle and ammunition would cause problems and it was claimed it would require over two years to reach the same production levels as the M14. Additional comparative testing was ordered. A small scandal erupted when it was revealed that an Infantry Board memo directed, "conduct only those tests that will reflect adversely on the AR-15." At the end of the year an evaluation was released and the AR-15 was condemned for the water in the bore issue, reliability, and reduced range and penetration. However, AR-15 shot groups on targets were half the size of M14 groups. The following recommendations were made and it is apparent that even then the AR-15 was being considered for Army-wide adoption:

The M16 replaced the 7.62mm M14 rifle through the 1970s. Pictured here is the M14A1 automatic rifle featuring a straight line butt stock, rear pistol grip, forward handgrip, M2 bipod, and muzzle compensator. Regardless of all these enhancements, designed to provide a more stable full-automatic weapon, it was still highly inaccurate, overheated due to its light barrel, and its 20-round magazine was inadequate for sustained fire. (Trey Moore collection)

- Continue the use of the M14 in units in Europe and units earmarked for Europe.
- Perform slow conversion from M1 to M14 in other areas. Final decision can be based on the experiences of AR-15 equipped units.
- Correct AR-15 reliability and night-firing deficiencies.
- Issue the AR-15 to airborne, airmobile, and Special Forces units.
- Issue M14E2 (M14A1) automatic rifles to M14-equipped units only.
- Continue development of other advanced weapons.

Comparative studies of the AR-15, M14, and other weapons were continued by different agencies. Allegations of unfair test requirements continued as well: M1 rifle requirements for ranges out to 800 yards, M14 match-grade rifles and ammunition used against AR-15s with standard ammunition, the AR-15 given a rain test when the M14 was not, the AR-15 required to fire full-automatic only while the M14 was fired semi-automatic, and the M14's negative aspects downplayed or omitted while the AR-15's faults were inflated. Much of the resistance to the AR-15 was because of the Army's 1962 Special Purpose Individual Weapon (SPIW) Project in which much faith was placed. This involved light selective-fire weapons firing .17cal (4.32mm) flechette rounds. Proponents were so confident of the program's success that they predicted that such a rifle would be standardized in 1966. The project was finally scrapped in 1972.

Scores of changes to the AR-15 and its ammunition were recommended through 1963. The change from 1-in-14in twist rifling to 1-in-12in solved some ballistics problems. The twist rate was critical to optimize the velocity of the bullet according to weight and length. One critical recommendation that was rejected was to chrome-plate the bore and chamber. If there was ever a weapon demanding a chromed bore and chamber, it was the M16; the M14 had a chromed chamber and bore. This would have alleviated some of the M16's problems, made cleaning easier, and prolonged barrel life. There was great debate regarding the ammunition and much testing. The bullet design, propellant, and other details could not be agreed on. At this time the AR-15's round was called the 5.64mm rather than the 5.56mm, as it was actually .224cal, even though it would be called .223. At this time the Air Force had 8,500 AR-15s, ordered another 19,000, and wanted 80,000 within five years. The Army had only 338, but forecast a need for a one-time purchase of 85,000 for airborne, airmobile, and Special Forces in 1964. The Secretary of Defense Robert McNamara approved purchase of the AR-15 in February 1963 as an interim procurement until the SPIW was fielded in the future. The request of Military Assistance Command, Vietnam (MACV – formerly MAAG-V) for 10,000 AR-15s was ignored.

The following month a joint services requirement for AR-15s and ammunition was approved so long as modifications and costs were kept to a minimum. After testing, the Marines concluded that the AR-15 and M14 were essentially equal in training, reliability and combat effectiveness, but that the AR-15 was lighter, easier to handle, and required less training. There was a complaint that no machine gun of the same caliber was available. Adoption was not recommended until such a weapon was available to replace the M60. This would have been a serious mistake as it would have lost the longer range and penetration capability of the 7.62mm. This is when the Marines began looking at the 5.56mm Stoner 63 light machine gun[2] (the Marines never adopted the dismal M14A1 automatic rifle).

[2] Military designations for the Stoner 63 were: US Navy, Mk 23 (LMG configuration); US Army, XM22 (rifle configuration), XM23 (SMG configuration), XM207 (LMG configuration)

In March 1963 the Army was designated the procurement agency for all users of the AR-15 and ammunition and an AR-15 project office was established. Colt would be the sole source contractor. It was at this time that the bolt-closure device, or forward assist device (a plunger-like device on the receiver's right side that ensured the bolt was fully closed and locked) was requested by the Army but opposed by the Air Force, while the Marines and Navy considered it non-essential. Its inclusion was rejected, another serious mistake. As the fielding plan developed it was directed that Colt and Eugene Stoner be consulted before implementing any changes. The Army conducted negotiations with Colt and Fairchild. Negotiations included the price of bayonets, bipods, cleaning gear, and spare parts. One issue was negotiated out of the contract: Fairchild would not receive a 15 percent royalty on spare parts. Authority was granted for the procurement of 28 million rounds of 5.56mm.

In September 1963 the Army type-classified the AR-15 as the "rifle, 5.56mm, XM16E1" and as "limited standard": in other words, for special purpose use. At the same time, the "cartridge, ball, 5.56mm, M193" was standardized (see page 51). The military dragged its feet on negotiations and the feud regarding the bolt assist and issues about slam firing (the weapon inadvertently firing when the bolt closed) led to Colt threatening to dismantle the AR-15 production line unless orders were received and production resumed. Finally, in November a US$13,300,000 contract was awarded to Colt for 85,000 XM16E1s for the Army and Marines and 19,000 M16s for the Air Force. Production was to run from May 1964 to April 1965. Eleven modifications were made prior to production. Just before production began the bolt forward assist device (FAD) was finally authorized for the XM16E1, but not the M16. It is often incorrectly stated that the XM16E1 lacked the forward assist. The contract was amended several times and the number of rifles increased to 201,000. An additional 78 million rounds of 5.56mm were ordered.

Problems plagued the M16 program with Colt experiencing quality control problems, constant debates over ammunition issues (chamber pressures, propellant types, bullet design), and the use of bolts lacking

Two lane controllers (wearing yellow helmets) coach an infantry Advanced Individual Training rifle squad as they conduct a live-fire assault course. Note the man with an XM3 bipod serving as a squad "automatic rifleman." An M16 with a bipod firing full-automatic was no substitute for a real automatic rifle or light machine gun. (Ft Polk Museum)

drain holes. Regardless, the Army commenced issuing the XM16E1 in May 1963. While there were occasional gun magazine and newspaper articles about the M16, the first sight many civilians had of the AR-15 was in the motion picture *Seven Days in May*, released in February 1964. It was not long before Colt was receiving enquiries from civilians about whether the new rifle was available for commercial sale.

THE XM16E1 DESCRIBED

The XM16E1 was unlike any rifle previously in use and contained many unique features. The AR-15 was often described as "futuristic" when introduced and many were enamored of its appearance, which is not a good way to rate a weapon. The upper and lower receivers were 6061 aircraft-grade aluminum alloy to reduce weight and resist corrosion. Components were anodized and phosphate coated. The barrel, bolt and carrier, and other internal parts were steel. The only component that rusted easily was the ejection port cover. The fiberglass-reinforced plastic stock, handguard, and pistol grip did not warp or splinter and further reduced weight. The stock's fiberglass shell contained a rigid plastic foam core. It was designed to be easily disassembled and repaired. The XM16E1 had approximately 100 parts (the AK-47 had about 130, and the M14 just over 70). No special tools were required for field disassembly. A bullet tip was used to adjust the front and rear sights and the magazine-release tension. The rifle's straight-line stock design without the traditional curve in the small of the stock allowed the barrel, bolt and carrier, and recoil buffer to be perfectly aligned horizontally. This eliminated the fulcrum created by traditional "bent" stocks to reduce muzzle climb. The use of a small-caliber cartridge with light propellant change and bullet further reduced muzzle climb and recoil. This made the weapon more accurate at longer ranges than most period assault rifles such as the AK-47.

The original XM16E1 had a three-prong flash suppressor that served as a muzzle compensator to slightly reduce recoil. The flash suppressor had a 21mm outside diameter allowing NATO standard rifle grenades to

XM16E1 rifle characteristics*

Caliber	5.56×45mm
Overall length	986mm (38.8in)
Barrel length	546mm (21.25in)
Weight without magazine	2.88kg (6.35lb)
Magazine	20-round straight
Cyclic rate	750–850rpm
Mode of fire	semi- & full-automatic
Muzzle velocity	970m/s (3,185fps)
Effective range	460m (500yd)

* The characteristics of the original AR-15 and the Air Force's M16 were virtually identical.

be fired without the need for a separate grenade launcher. A simple ladder-type grenade sight could be clipped to the front sight frame. The front sight was set on a triangular-shaped frame (cross-sight gate) fixed to the barrel with the gas vent, bayonet lug, and front sling swivel as part of it. The thin stainless steel gas tube ran from its fitting in the front sight frame above the barrel to the receiver where it interfaced with the small tubular gas port, called the gas key, atop the bolt carrier. The small bolt was held in the large bolt carrier and the T-shaped charging handle was linked to it with the handle positioned to the rear of the carrying handle base. On the left finger grip of the "T" was a release latch that had to be depressed to pull the charging handle to the rear. This replaced the original AR-15's trigger-like cocking lever inside the carrying handle's forward end.

The ejection port was on the right side and protected by a spring-loaded cover that automatically opened when the weapon was fired. It had to be manually closed, though. The magazine release button was on the right side below the ejection port and above the trigger. The bolt forward assist device was a plunger-like affair fitted in a housing integral to the right rear of the upper receiver. Punched with the palm of the hand after chambering the first round or clearing a misfire, it ensured the bolt was locked fully forward (AR-15s and M16s lacked the forward assist). The spring-loaded plunger with an oval head would strike one of the 28 serrations cut in the right side of the bolt carrier to force it forward into a locked position if the return spring failed to force it sufficiently forward to lock.

The selector lever was on the left side above the pistol grip (SAFE, SEMI-AUTO, AUTO). Above the trigger guard on the left side was the bolt release catch, which allowed the bolt to be held to the rear after the last shot was fired from a magazine. When depressed the bolt ran forward to chamber a round from a fresh magazine. On the lower receiver – front-to-rear – were the magazine well, the trigger (the lower trigger guard arm was hinged to swing rearward against the pistol grip to allow firing with gloved hands), and a hollow pistol grip. The trigger/hammer group was similar to that used in the M1 and M14 rifles. Atop the receiver was the integral carrying handle with the rear sight. The rear sight was adjustable for elevation and windage. It was a flip-type sight with two peep apertures

BELOW LEFT
Detail of an M16A1 rifle showing the rear sight adjustment on the upper rear end of the carrying handle, T-shaped charging handle grip, and forward assist device (FAD). The ejection port cover is open showing the bolt carrier. The small notches are some of the 28 that caught the FAD plunger when punched to ensure the carrier was rammed fully forward. The magazine release fencing (the surrounding ridge preventing accidental release) is seen above the forward end of the trigger guard. (Courtesy of David Trentham)

BELOW
The left side of the receiver of an M16A1 rifle produced by General Motors Hydra-Matic. The horizontal bar on the magazine well is part of the magazine release. Above it is a bolt release lever that allowed the open bolt to run forward after inserting a loaded magazine. The selector lever is set on Safe. Turning the lever vertically set it on Semi-automatic and moving it to the rear sets it on Full-automatic. The word FULL is covered by the lever. The straight retaining ring on the rear of the handguard was difficult to pull to the rear to remove the two handguard halves. This was corrected on the M16A2 and later models. (Courtesy of David Trentham)

A US Special Forces captain passes through a village with his Civilian Irregular Defense Group Montagnard strikers, 1964. Special Forces were among the first US soldiers to use XM16E1 rifles in Vietnam. (Larry Burrows/ Time Life Pictures/Getty Images)

providing the shooter with a choice. The front post sight was adjustable for elevation. Both the front and rear sights were protected by guards. The carrying handle could also mount a telescope or night vision sight ("starlightscope").

The foam-filled butt stock contained the recoil buffer – officially the recoil spring guide (called an Edgewater buffer by collectors). This prevented a folding stock from being used and restricted future shortened versions (XM177, M4) to telescoping stocks. There was a hard, rubber-like plastic recoil pad on the butt. The AR-15, M16, XM16E1, and early M16A1 rifles lacked a butt stowage compartment for cleaning gear. The rear sling swivel was on the lower end (heel) of the butt. The handguard was two-part and could be removed by pulling back on a spring-loaded retaining ring on its rear end. The guards' insides were lined with aluminum heat-reflecting shields, which also reinforced the guards. There were small cooling slots in the top and bottom of the handguard. The unique triangular handguard tapered to a smaller size forward. It allowed a person with small hands to hold the weapon easily by sliding his hand forward until he achieved a comfortable grip. Initially only 20-round staggered-row box magazines were available. The magazines were lightweight alloy and care had to be taken not to damage them. Magazines of other alloys and plastics were tested.

On the plus side the M16 was light, compact, and easy to handle. Training in its operation, disassembly, and firing techniques was easy. Much more 5.56mm ammunition could be carried than 7.62mm. It was reasonably accurate to 460m and achieved satisfactory wounds up to 400m. It was stable during full-automatic fire, but nonetheless accuracy beyond 100m was questionable.

FIELDING THE XM16E1

There were mixed reviews of the XM16E1 in the hands of troops prior to deploying to Vietnam. Many liked its light weight and handiness, ease of operation, and firepower. It was realized by most that automatic fire was only suitable in special circumstances and was inaccurate at longer ranges. The most common complaint was its apparent fragility. In contrast to the heavy and extremely robust M1 and M14 rifles, the little black rifle seemed more akin to a toy and it was soon dubbed the "Mattel Toy rifle" after the well-known toy manufacturer. (A myth emerged that M16s were actually produced by Mattel Toy Company, but this is a hoax, as is Photoshopped "proof" of receiver markings.) It was also called the "plastic rifle" and the "black magic."

In March 1965, recruits undergoing airborne infantry training at Ft Gordon, Georgia, were the first training unit to receive XM16E1s. In the early summer Colt ran out of the recommended IMR powder-loaded ammunition and XM16E1s could no longer pass acceptance tests. This caused production to be suspended. Even with the rifle's emerging problems, in July General William Westmoreland, commanding MACV, asked for a study examining the possibility of issuing the XM16E1 to all US troops in Vietnam. In August 1965 work began on a 30-round magazine. This experienced many difficulties as the deep magazine well required the upper end to be straight and the lower curved; in addition, the rifles' wells were irregularly dimensioned due to poor quality control. Late in the year small numbers of M16s and XM16E1s were ordered as replacements, issued to the Coast Guard, and the replaced rifles were given

Vietnam-era M16 weapons

Military designation	Using services	Colt model	Production
AR-15 rifle	USAF	601	1959–63
AR-15 rifle	USAF	602	1963–64
M16 rifle	USAF	604	1964–65, 1970
XM16E1 rifle	Army, Marines	603	1964–67
M16A1 rifle	Army, Marines	603	1967–82
Mk 4 Mod 0 rifle	Navy	604 modified	c.1970/71
XM177 SMG	Army	610	1966
XM177E1 SMG	Army	609	1967–68
XM177E2 SMG	Army	629	1967–70
GAU-5/A SMG	USAF	649	(not known)
GAU-5/A/A SMG	USAF	630	(not known)
GAU-5/A/B SMG	USAF	629 (XM177E2)	1967–70
GAU-5/P SMG	USAF	610 (XM177)	1966

The USAF designated SMG versions GAU: GA = Airborne Gun, U = Unit. Actually, being a shoulder-fired weapon, it does not fit in the GAU category and it is not known why this designation was assigned. It is usually assigned to aircraft-mounted guns. It does not mean "Gun, Automatic, Unit," invented to provide an explanation of the GAU code.

to Australia. In December, Westmoreland, with the Marine Corps in accord, requested 180,000 XM16E1s for both services, 106,000 for the ARVN, and 9,000 for the Koreans to be delivered as soon as possible. Colt was told to double its production to 16,000 per month and ammunition production was expanded. The Department of Defense added another 123,000 rifles for military assistance programs and in all 115 million rounds of ammunition were ordered.

In early 1966 the need for a submachine-gun version of the M16 was stated. These would be used by MACV-SOG (Studies and Observation Group) conducting covert cross-border reconnaissance missions inside Laos and Cambodia and possibly to replace some pistols in infantry units. SOG had been using Swedish-made Carl Gustav 9mm m/45b submachine guns ("Swedish K"), but Sweden had declared an arms embargo against the USA in protest against the Vietnam War. In early 1966 Colt was informed to expect orders for up to 400,000 rifles. Ammunition demands were increased to 150 million a month. Orders for 2,050 XM177E1 submachine guns were made in early 1966, which had been type-classified from the CAR-15. In February all infantry replacements in the States began receiving XM16E1 training and the Marines began XM16E1 procurement. The 1966 procurement plan for M16s was 483,000 for all services. This would be increased to 808,000 XM16E1 rifles, 29,000 M16s, and 2,800 XM177s. There was consideration and debate about finding a second manufacturer to increase the delivery rate. Ammunition with the improved propellant began to arrive in June and an improved buffer was approved.

All Army maneuver units in Vietnam were issued the XM16E1 by August. Many support and service units still had the M14 and it would be some time before they received XM16E1s. In September the closed-end "birdcage" four-slot flash suppressor was approved. The prong-type

Basic trainees in the early 1970s receiving introduction training on the M16A1 rifle, one seeming a bit bored with the lecture. Prior to this basic trainees used 7.62mm M14 rifles, while M16 training took place in infantry Advanced Individual Training from 1969. (Ft Polk Museum)

snagged on limbs and vines (a significant nuisance), easily broke, and helped water bleed into the bore. In November 1966 the Chief of Staff of the Army recommended that the XM16E1 be adopted as Standard A for Army-wide issue, but that the M14 and M14A1 too should remain Standard A until fully replaced by XM16E1s. A comparable 5.56mm squad automatic should not be adopted, even though the need for such a weapon was generally recognized as early as 1966. The XM177, replacing some pistols and rifles, and XM149 grenade launcher should also be adopted. Product improvement of the XM16E1 should continue and be incorporated incrementally into production rifles. The first 2,000 XM177s were delivered that same month.

PROBLEMS EMERGE

The airborne and airmobile troops deploying to Vietnam in 1965 had been training with the XM16E1 in the States and were very familiar with the weapon's nuances, including the special cleaning needs. Regardless of the extensive testing and modifications made over the past seven years, deficiencies soon began to appear in actual extended combat under harsh climate conditions.

The 173d Airborne Brigade; 1st Brigade, 101st Airborne Division; and 1st Cavalry Division were the first three Army major combat units deployed to Vietnam in 1965 and were armed with the XM16E1. The first Marine units arriving in Vietnam were armed with M14s, as were the Army's 1st, 25th, and 4th Infantry Divisions. Later Army units arrived with XM16E1/M16A1 rifles: the 9th Infantry Division, the various separate brigades that would comprise the Americal Division, and the rest of the 101st Airborne Division as well as other separate brigades. The first light infantry brigade to deploy, the 196th in August 1966, had trained with M14s, but received XM16E1s before boarding ship. Of the early

A recruit executes a butt stroke against a bayonet dummy. The XM16E1 rifle with an M7 bayonet, or any M16 variant, made for a poor bayonet fighting weapon. It was too light, insufficiently robust, and even had a rubber-padded butt. The M1 and M14 rifles, being some 2–3lb heavier than the M16, had steel butt plates. In 2010 the Army eliminated bayonet instruction, replacing it with expedient weapons and other close-combat techniques. The Marines, however, have retained bayonet training. (Ft Polk Museum)

deploying units, only the 1st Cavalry Division did not report serious problems with the M16. The Marines, too, initially reported no problems, but this was reported by higher headquarters and not the troop units.

Most Marine units began receiving the XM16E1 in April 1967 and immediately experienced problems arising from several factors. Most units received little if any cleaning gear beyond some cleaning rods and bore brushes. Some units had never heard of chamber brushes. Colt is said to have hyped the weapon as futuristic, requiring little maintenance owing to new materials. This was interpreted to mean the black rifle was "self-cleaning." Few units conducted meaningful functional and maintenance training and technical manuals were scarce. There were complaints that the forward assist device did no good in clearing jams – in fact, it was not meant to. Poor cleaning, rapid fire, and fouling led to chamber pitting. The pitting filled with oil, dust, sand, and propellant residue, causing cases to stick. This resulted in higher chamber pressure, which led to higher cyclic rates. This further resulted in jams, failures to extract, double-feeds, and rim-sheers. This last saw the extractor pulling off part of the rim, leaving the case in the chamber. The only way to remove the case was to punch it out using a cleaning rod, if the rifleman had one. Broken extractors and extractor springs were also problems. There were reports of men found dead beside partly disassembled weapons, as the weapon had to be opened and the bolt carrier removed to punch out the stuck case with a cleaning rod.

Several problems contributed to these issues. The first was the failure to chrome-plate the chamber. Under the high heat conditions, extensive rapid fire, and higher cyclic rates, the chamber quickly pitted or eroded. The use of improper oil and lubricants gummed it even more and, coupled with poor or no cleaning, quickly led to frequent stoppages.

During the Hill Fights outside of Khe Sanh in the spring of 1967 the Marines first encountered widespread problems with the XM16E1. A Marine officer, Dick Culver, reported:

> The [1st] Force Service Regiment sent a trouble shooting team to visit us aboard the LPH [landing ship, helicopter] shortly after the Hill Fights to try and pin down the problem. As soon as the ordnance team arrived, they made it clear that *they* were already well informed (meaning they'd already made up their minds) concerning our problem and had decided (without so much as a question to us) that *we* as a Battalion were responsible for a bad rap being given to a marvelous little rifle! The lads in the rear had decided that *we* were simply not keeping our rifles clean, and if we weren't such inattentive and unmotivated "oafs" being led by incompetents, we wouldn't *have* such a problem. Needless to say, the hackles stood up on the back of our necks.

Not long after the arrival of combat units in Vietnam, complaints began to pour in from the Marines and Army. A great deal of understandable bitterness was expressed by combat troops through official and unofficial channels. Various Army and Marine agencies conducted endless studies and investigations; there were Congressional hearings and scathing newspaper articles including endless first-hand accounts and photos of dead Americans with disassembled M16s. One study reported that 50 percent of interviewed troops experienced malfunctions, usually failures to extract. Stuck cases, broken extractors and springs, and jammed selector levers were common – though a new "lubricant, small arms" (LSA) was issued and proved to be effective.

The real culprit was the propellant ordered by the Chief of Ordnance. The Army successfully used ball powder in all of its ammunition. This was more prone to fouling, but had little effect on weapons like the M14 rifle and M60 machine gun. The M16, though, had a sensitive gas system which directed the gas down the very narrow tube over the barrel directly to the bolt carrier – direct impingement. There was no conventional operating rod or gas piston to "block" propellant residue from fouling the entire tube and system. This meant that propellant residue was vented into the receiver and built up rapidly on the bolt and carrier, as well as fouling the gas tube. This system reduced the number of parts and weight, but with the wrong kind of propellant it was a recipe for disaster.

The direct impingement system uses hot gas fed from the barrel down the gas tube into the receiver where it enters the gas key atop the bolt carrier. Gas is vented through the gas key into a cavity inside the bolt carrier where the gas expands and pressure causes the bolt carrier to be driven back against the initially stationary bolt. The carrier's rearward movement is transferred into the rotation of the bolt via a cam slot in the bolt carrier attached to the bolt. As the bolt rotates to unlock from the barrel breech, the bolt carrier continues its rearward travel under the residual pressure in the barrel to extract the spent case and compress the buffer return spring in the butt. The return spring forces the forward movement of the bolt carrier, which strips a cartridge from the magazine and rotates the bolt to lock into the breech. The bolt has eight radial locking lugs, one of which is on the extractor. Fouling builds up extensively in the rear portion of the gas tube, the gas key, the bolt and carrier, and inside the receiver, all difficult to reach for cleaning.

Stoner had recommended a commercial propellant called Improved Military Rifle (IMR) powder, with tiny cylindrical particles. It was slightly more expensive, and this made a difference when millions of rounds were procured; in addition, large ball powder stocks existed. The ammunition used by the Army to test the AR-15 came from the 8.5 million rounds procured by the Air Force, and was loaded with IMR powder. This gave good results, but it was found that IMR powder caused erratic chamber pressures and muzzle velocities. After a great deal of hot debate the Army decided on ball powder, a disaster in the making. *After* making the decision the Army approached Stoner, asking if this was a good decision. They had hoped for his reassurance; instead, Stoner stated that any change in the ammunition affected a weapon's performance, and refused to endorse the change.

Not only did ball powder lead to excessive fouling, it increased the cyclic rate above the maximum allowable 850rpm, up to 1,000rpm. This increased breakages and malfunctions. To allow a higher percentage of rifles to be accepted during proof-firing, Colt convinced the Army to up the allowable rate to 900rpm and to allow acceptance test firing with IMR-loaded ammunition, even though ball powder was issued in combat. This did nothing to alleviate the problems when these "acceptable" weapons were issued to the troops. The Combat Developments Experimentation Center conducted comparative tests between the M16, M14, Stoner 63, and captured AK-47s (the US weapons were new). The hard-used AK-47s proved superior and it was fully realized that the use of ball powder in M16s was the problem. The Army refused to admit this and rather than changing the powder decided to design a heavier recoil buffer – making the rifle accommodate inadequate ammunition rather than improving the ammunition. An XM16E1 field manual was finally released in January 1965.

There were magazine problems as well. Bent or spread lips prevented or hampered feeding. Magazines, which did not rust, were often oiled, and some of this oil worked its way inside. Cartridges, too, were oiled. This attracted dust, sand, and vegetation debris, creating a gummy gunk. When chambered in a hot weapon oiled cartridges picked up more fouling in the chamber, which was a further cause of jams. A directive was issued not to oil cartridges, only to clean them dry. Rough treatment was normal and the magazine lips might be compressed, which would prevent feeding, or spread, leading to double-feeds. There were instances when 21 rounds were inadvertently jammed in. Dents in the sides also jammed the magazine. Most troops loaded only 18 or 19 rounds to reduce follower spring strain and jamming because of too much tension.

THE M16 EXPOSED

5.56mm M16A1 assault rifle

1 Buttstock
2 Receiver extension
3 Action spring
4 Recoil buffer
5 Charging handle
6 Forward assist assembly
7 Rear sight adjuster
8 Rear sight
9 Carrying handle
10 Hammer
11 Sear
12 Disconnector
13 Disconnector spring
14 Trigger spring
15 Trigger
16 Hinged trigger guard
17 Magazine release button
18 Magazine follower spring
19 Magazine follower plate
20 20-round magazine
21 Bolt carrier
22 Gas key
23 Firing pin
24 Bolt
25 Gas tube
26 Gas port
27 Handguard
28 Front sight
29 Bayonet lug
30 Flash suppressor
31 Forward sling swivel
32 M7 bayonet knife
33 M8A1 bayonet scabbard
34 Magazine loading clip guide
35 5.56mm NATO ten-round loading clip
36 M1 sling
37 Pistol grip
38 Rear sling swivel

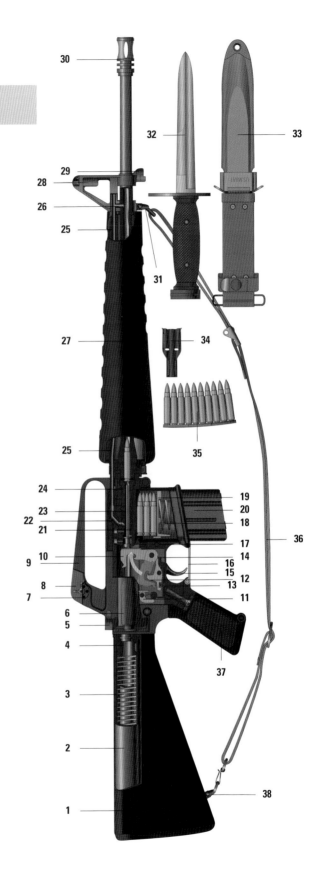

A basic trainee fires the M16A1 rifle under the very direct supervision of a drill sergeant in a posed photo (note no magazine inserted). Trainees were taught to fire from standing, kneeling, squatting, sitting, and prone positions as well as various supported positions such as the prone supported shown here. (Ft Polk Museum)

Units that had trained with the M16 Stateside before deploying had less trouble. There was time there to clean weapons properly, and there was apparently more cleaning gear available. The opportunity existed to clean weapons after qualification range firing and live-fire exercises and to turn them into arms rooms, not at all like field conditions in Vietnam. It was not until October 1966 that the Army Weapons Command dispatched a team to train instructors in every brigade who would in turn properly train their own troops. It was found that most weapons were inadequately cleaned and suffered from erosion, corrosion, excessive fouling, and too much or too little of proper lubricants. One field study reported that improper lubricants and cleaning agents were used: "solvents, gasoline, JP-4 aircraft fuel, diesel oil, motor oil, LPS [lubricant], WD-40,[3] Dri-Slide, MIL-L-46000 [weapon lubricant], insect repellant, and water." Many had frozen buffers, which led to excessive wear and high cyclic rates.

From the end of 1966 it became mandatory for replacements arriving in Vietnam to receive two hours of maintenance training and the new 32-page comic-book-like preventive maintenance pamphlet was distributed in 1968. Consideration was being given to either replacing the

[3] It was not known at the time, but WD-40, a penetrating lubricant, can penetrate cartridge primer pockets causing them to misfire

M79 grenadiers' M1911A1 pistol with an M16 or submachine-gun version, or arming the grenadiers with the XM148 grenade launcher mounted on an XM16E1. At the end of December 1966 the first XM148s arrived in Vietnam, but their issue was limited through the war. In July 1967 the Army received manufacturing rights for the M16 from Colt, a step toward contracting another manufacturer. Almost 400 Colt/Realist 3× telescopes were sent to Vietnam in March 1967, not for sniper rifles, but for specialist marksmen.

When in 1970 it was decided to replace the M14 rifles in Europe, there was a great deal of controversy about the USA reneging on the 7.62mm NATO standardization agreement – STANAG 2310, ratified in 1957. It seemed that after the USA had leaned heavily on some participants to accept the cartridge, now it wanted to change over to a new round. However, it was seldom pointed out that the standardization agreement had expired in January 1968. In March 1968 all countries of the NATO Standardization Panel voted to undertake testing to consider the 5.56mm as an additional NATO cartridge. By the end of that year the Army possessed over 275,000 M16s. In February 1969, MACV recommended issuing 268,000 M16A1s to the South Vietnamese Regional and Popular

The Colt-designed 40mm XM148 under-barrel grenade launcher. It was intended to replace the standalone shoulder-fired M79 grenade launcher in order to provide the grenadier with a point-fire and area-fire weapon, and a better self-defense weapon than a pistol. The problem-ridden weapon was replaced by the XM203. (Trey Moore collection)

A detail view of the XM148 grenade launcher. Note the special handguard required to mount the weapon on the M16A1. It saw some combat testing in Vietnam, which revealed its many defects. The trigger can be seen at the barrel's breech end just forward of the magazine well. (Trey Moore collection)

Forces once the regular ARVN was rearmed. In May another troop survey revealed:

- A quarter of personnel still lubricated ammunition.
- The buffer replacement was not complete.
- Over a quarter of personnel had not received M16 training when arriving in Vietnam and another quarter had not received any before deploying.
- 10 percent had not zeroed their weapon and 30 percent had not re-zeroed within three months.
- Almost 20 percent reported that their units did not test-fire weapons.
- Most cleaned weapons daily, but cleaned magazines and ammunition only weekly.
- There were periodic shortages of cleaning gear and supplies.

THE M16A1 RIFLE

In January 1967, the XM16E1 was classified as Standard A and redesignated "rifle, 5.56mm, M16A1."[4] This was after a great deal of modification and improved parts. Changes were made in the XM16E1's specifications through its entire production run and by the time it was declared Standard A it was a very different rifle. Earlier production rifles

---

[4] The M16A1 did not replace the M16 as is often assumed. It superseded the XM16E1, from which the M16A1 evolved. The M16 remained standard for the Air Force

[5] Company L, 3d Battalion, 1st Marines was issued Stoner 63 rifles, carbines, and machine guns for testing from March to May 1967; these weapons were replaced by M16A1s owing to excessive malfunctions

were depot upgraded with new parts. In April all Marine infantry and reconnaissance units in Vietnam were issued the M16A1,[5] while the ARVN received sufficient M16A1s to arm its airborne and Marine battalions. In the States all Vietnam-oriented infantry training centers were conducting all live-fire training with the XM16E1, but some had Air Force M16s to release XM16E1s to Vietnam. Chrome-plated firing pins and chambers, but not bores, were approved for the M16A1 in May.

In June 742,000 more M16s and M16A1s were ordered. In July the new MACV commander, General Creighton Abrams, canceled further issue of M2 carbines to the ARVN, with the M2 to be replaced by the M16A1. At the end of 1968, M16A1 production by two additional manufacturers was authorized; they were Harrington and Richardson (H&R) of Worchester, Massachusetts and Hydra-Matic Division of General Motors Corporation at Detroit, Michigan. Both produced rifles from 1969 to 1971.

At the beginning of 1969 authorization was granted to provide 516,000 M16A1s to South Vietnam. M16s had been or would be provided to Laos, Thailand, Korea, and the Philippines and later to Cambodia. Colt delivered its one millionth M16 rifle that year.

By March 1970 all infantry training centers were equipped with M16A1 rifles; these were used in infantry Advanced Individual Training, although Basic Combat Training units still had M14s. In 1970 M16A1s began to be delivered to National Guard units and issue continued through 1972. In summer 1970 M16A1s began to be issued to US troops dedicated to NATO. In October an order for 742,000 rifles was awarded to Colt as the decision was made to issue the M16A1 to Army and Marine forces worldwide. Beginning in 1971 all M16s were produced with chrome-lined bores and chambers. M16A1 issue to Vietnam, Cambodia, Laos, Indonesia, and Jordan continued or was initiated and deliveries continued through 1975. Also in 1971 the National Board for the Promotion of Rifle Practice allowed M16s and AR-15s to compete in National Matches, the military-wide annual competition.

The M16A1 was a much-upgraded XM16E1 and outwardly looked little different from the early model. Important, but less apparent, was the fact that Colt switched from 6061 aircraft-grade aluminum alloy for the receiver to 7075 in 1968 as it was less affected by humid climates and sweaty hands, and this remains in use. It must be pointed out that the improved parts can be found in both XM16E1s and M16A1s with a myriad of changes made between 1964 and 1967. Improved parts continued to be developed for the rest of the M16A1's service life. There were periods where mixes of both old and new parts in any combination could be found in factory weapons. Mixes of parts were also found in weapons in the field as parts were replaced either during unit repairs or depot rebuilds. For example, in 1968/69 most XM16E1s received new bolt carriers and birdcage suppressors.

The new buffer, which slowed the recoil, was approved in 1966 along with the "birdcage" type flash suppressor, but prong-type suppressors could still be found, for example on early M16A1s. Up until 1965 the bolt

carrier and bolt were chromed, between 1966 and 1967 both chromed and Parkerized bolts and carriers were fitted, and after 1967 all were Parkerized. Smaller parts were improved to include: firing pin, firing pin retaining pin, selector lever and pins, disconnector, and lower receiver extensions. Lower receivers were provided with an extended "fencing" ridge protecting the magazine release. From 1966 to 1967–68 barrels lacked chrome bores and chambers, and from 1969 to 1970–71 the chamber alone was chromed. Barrels with chromed bores and chambers were produced from 1971. In 1970 a butt storage compartment for cleaning gear was provided, along with a more rigid butt filler material.

In April 1970 the Navy type-classified a version of the M16A1 for the SEALs, the "rifle, 5.56mm, Mk 4 Mod 0." It was fitted with a Mk 2 Mod 0 (HEL M4A) suppressor, coated with thermally cured gray Kal-Gard® Gun-Kote to protect against seawater and corrosion, a drain hole through the stock from the buffer, and buffer sealing ring. Submersion to 200ft did not damage the weapon. There was an inoperable M16A1 "demil" (demilitarized) used for training and drills as well as a full-weight hard plastic mockup with an actual worn-out barrel.

XM177-SERIES SUBMACHINE GUNS

Colt began development of CAR-15 (Colt Automatic Rifle) carbines and submachine guns in 1964, resulting in a military version generally known as the "Colt Commando" or "shorty 16." The Army type-classified the CAR-15 "submachine gun, 5.56mm, XM177 and XM177E1" (Colt

The black rifle in Vietnam, 1972 (previous pages)

The widespread introduction of the M16 rifle in Vietnam gave it a lasting reputation, some good, much bad. Besides the early problem-riddled XM16E1, the most widely used version was the M16A1 – the standard rifle for most US and Free World forces. The rifleman on the ground has attached an XM3 "cloth pin" bipod to his M16A1. Although little used by this time, they were handy for stable firing. The elongated case on the rifleman's side held the bipod and cleaning gear. He carries a 2oz bottle of lubricant, small arms (LSA), especially formulated for the M16, conveniently in his helmet band. The platoon leader (left) carries an XM177E2 submachine gun. Owing to a surplus of the weapons because of the drawdown of Special Forces covert reconnaissance units, the 1st Cavalry Division (Airmobile) was issued them for company officers, where it was generally called the CAR-15 or Colt Commando. Most soldiers removed their slings as they made noise, snagged on vegetation, and the rifle needed to be carried at the ready. This officer has attached his sling without using the sling swivels, a popular manner that was quieter. The 40mm under-barrel M203 grenade launcher, first field-tested in 1968 and standardized in August 1969, was in widespread use by 1970. Here, though, the grenadier (right) is armed with the less effective Colt-designed XM148 grenade launcher, which was plagued by parts breakage and poor sights, and was difficult to cock. Grenadiers generally carried less rifle ammunition than other troops as their primary weapon was the grenade launcher. Besides the four-magazine belt pouches, most riflemen carried one or two bandoliers with seven magazines each. Many did not use pouches at all.

A Combat Control Team (CCT) member participates in a training exercise at Hurlburt Field, Florida, home of the 1st Special Operations Wing. The GAU-5/A/A submachine gun was the Air Force version of the Army's XM177E2, but lacked the forward assist device (FAD) to the rear of the ejection port. The GAU-5/A/B had an FAD. (USAF)

Models 610 and 609, respectively) in January 1967. Initial issue was completed in March. The Air Force version of the XM177 was known as the GAU-5/A; it lacked the forward assist while the Army XM177E1 had a forward assist, but both had 10in barrels. In April 1967 the new version with a barrel 1.5in longer was type-classified as the XM177E2 (Colt Model 629). This reduced muzzle blast and flash, and allowed an XM149 grenade launcher to be attached. The XM177E2 was issued to Special Forces reconnaissance projects, Mobile Strike Forces, and other special units to include the SEALs. Later, some infantry company-level officers, tracker dog teams, and Ranger long-range patrol companies in Vietnam received XM177E2s, which by no means entirely replaced M16A1s. XM177E2 production ceased in 1970.

XM177E2 submachine gun characteristics

Caliber	5.56×45mm
Overall length (retracted)	754mm (29.7in)
Overall length (extended)	838mm (33in)
Barrel length	292mm (11.5in) (381mm/15in with compensator)
Weight without magazine	2.76kg (6.1lb)
Magazine	20-round straight (30-round curved limited availability)
Cyclic rate	650–900rpm
Mode of fire	semi- & full-automatic
Muzzle velocity	844m/s (2,770fps)
Effective range	350m (380yd)

The Air Force called the XM177E2 the GAU-5/A/B. The GAU-5/A/A (Colt Model 630) was an XM177E2 without the forward assist. The Air Force made piecemeal upgrades to the GAU-5s and with the advent of the M855 ball in the 1980s they received 14.5in barrels with 1-in-7in twist and birdcage suppressors, and were redesignated as the GUU-5/P – the designation standing for gun, miscellaneous personal equipment.

The XM177 series were more than just M16s with shortened barrels and telescoping stocks. The shorter barrel and gas tube caused difficulties in perfecting the weapon's operation owing to the lesser amount of gas bleed into the gas tube. Muzzle blast and flash, recoil, control, and noise levels were increased. A special muzzle modulator was developed to overcome some of these problems and also served as a counterbalance, as the shortened weapon was unbalanced. The modulator was a 4.25in-long solid steel cylinder with flash suppressor slits at the muzzle. Internal cast chambers branched off the bore to bleed off gas in order to reduce the muzzle blast and noise level. The government declared this a "sound suppressor" even though it had no internal baffles or sound-absorbing materials like real silencers. It did serve to reduce the firing noise level, but only to that of the M16A1 rifle. Since the internal chambers were impossible to clean, with use its sound reduction capabilities gradually deteriorated. It also slightly reduced accuracy, which was already degraded by the short barrel, lower velocity, and shorter sight radius (distance between front and rear sights).

The XM177E2's upper and lower receiver groups and their operating and control features were the same as the M16A1's. The barrel was 11.5in long compared to the M16A1's 20in and was manufactured with chromed chambers. The triangular handguard was abandoned for a shorter round one. Rather than different right and left handguards, the XM177 series used interchangeable upper and lower handguards, which influenced the future M16A2. The telescoping stock contained a shorter recoil buffer. There was a sling swivel on the front sight frame, but no bayonet lug, and it could not launch rifle grenades. There was a slot atop the rear end of the butt for the sling and the butt locking latch was on its lower forward end. The submachine guns were supposed to be issued with seven 30-round magazines, but development difficulties were met and very few were issued.

40mm grenade launchers

The ability to attach 40mm grenade launchers to the M16 is an important addition to squad capabilities and is said to represent a third of the unit's firepower. The 40mm M79 shoulder-fired grenade launcher was standardized in 1960, and through the Vietnam War, where it became an iconic weapon, the Army issued two per rifle squad and the Marines one. The "thumper's" firepower contribution was recognized, but each M79 meant one less rifle in the squad, one less point-fire weapon. (The grenadier's pistol contributed nothing meaningful to unit firepower.) Development of an under-barrel 40mm grenade launcher that could be attached to an M16 rifle began in the mid-1960s. The first result was the Colt-designed XM148 of 1965. Issued for limited combat testing in Vietnam in 1967, it was plagued with mechanical and safety problems, the most annoying being that the barrel sometimes followed the projectile downrange. Additionally, the sight was defective, the trigger mechanism complex and easily broken, and an excessive 30lb force was necessary to cock it. Some units requested re-issue of the M79. The design of the XM203 Grenade Launcher Attachment Development (GLAD) was begun in 1967 by AAI Corporation and in April 1969 500 XM203s were issued to the 1st, 4th and 25th Infantry and 101st Airborne Divisions, and the 11th Armored Cavalry Regiment, for combat testing. It was standardized in August 1969. Colt did not begin series production until 1971 and it saw only limited use in Vietnam before the last combat unit was withdrawn in August 1972. With the advent of the M203 the Army retained two grenade launchers per squad, but the Marines assigned three, which remains the standard allocation. The "two-oh-three" can be mounted on the M16/M16A1/A2/A3/A4 rifles with a special handguard as well as unmodified M4 and M4A1 carbines with a special front attachment point. A modified version, the M203A1, has fittings to mount on the M4 and M4A1 carbines using the quick-mount adapter. The M203A2 is mounted on the M16A4 Modular Weapon System with Picatinny rails. The M203, M203A1, and M203A2 barrels are 12in long and weigh 3lb. It is often reported that the M203A1 has a 9in barrel. It does not; the 9in barrel assembly is a special shortened barrel provided in the M4A1 SOPMOD kit for Special Operations Forces requiring a less cumbersome weapon for close-combat ranges. The M203 grenade launcher can be mounted on M16-series rifles by the unit's armorer while the M203A1 must be mounted on the M4 carbine by the unit's supporting direct support maintenance company. The M203's range is 150m for point targets and 350m for area targets; the range is slightly shorter for the 9in SOPMOD M203. Minimum range is 14–27m to allow HE/HEDP rounds to arm at a safe distance. Rate of fire is 5–7rpm. Standard ammunition includes: HE, HEDP (high-explosive/dual-purpose – fragmentation and limited shaped-charge effect), buckshot, flechette, tear gas, various crowd dispersal munitions, and a wide range of colored smoke and pyrotechnic signal rounds.

The M203 will eventually be replaced by the 40mm M320 Grenade Launcher Module (GLM), adopted in 2008 and issued in mid-2009. It is based on the German H&K AG36. It weighs 3.3lb and has an 11in barrel. It can be used as a standalone launcher by adding a 1lb telescoping butt. Ranges and rates of fire are the same as the M203, but it handles better and has a greatly improved day/night sight and fire control including a handheld laser rangefinder. The barrel pivots to the left to allow longer special purpose rounds to be loaded.

BELOW An M4 carbine mounting a new 40mm M320 Grenade Launcher Module (GLM), adopted in 2008 and issued in mid-2009. The day/ night sight and fire control is fitted to the left side RAS tactical rail. It is based on the German H&K AG36 and will eventually replace the M203, which has been in use for the past 40 years. (US Army)

BEYOND VIETNAM

With the fall of South Vietnam in April 1975, over 946,000 M16-type weapons fell into communist hands. They appeared worldwide in communist-sponsored insurgencies and terrorist groups throughout the 1980s. Military production of M16A1s dropped off drastically after the Vietnam War. Purchases were made by countries like Chile, Ghana, Nicaragua, and Zaire, but these were only a few thousand apiece and Colt fell on hard times. However, Thailand was provided with 64,000 M16A1s in 1975. In mid-1975 the Korean Daewoo Precision Industries M16A1 plant became operational. Singapore had begun producing its version of the M16A1, the M16S1, in 1973. It was also sold to the Philippines and Thailand. Elisco Tool in the Philippines also produces the M16A1 as the M613P. US production did pick up somewhat in 1976–77 as the Army rebuilt after Vietnam. The new 30-round magazines were in general use by the mid-1970s. Colt produced only 12 of the M16A1's parts in-house; the rest were made by 70 subcontractors (including Diemaco/Colt Canada and ArmaLite) and assembled by Colt. Taiwan has produced an M16 variant called the Type 65 since 1976.

It was not until March 1972 that the Army stated a need for a 5.56mm squad automatic weapon. The Marines tested the M16 heavy barrel automatic rifle (HBAR) as a possible squad automatic, but dropped the project in 1977 as it overheated and was unable to maintain sustained fire. In 1978 the Army continued to search for a squad automatic weapon. One

These Malaysian marines are armed with a mix of M16A1 rifles and Austrian 5.56mm AUG rifles. The lead man's M16A1 is fitted with an M203 grenade launcher. The M16A1 is widely used in Asian countries. (US Navy)

contender was the 5.56mm FN Minimi, designated the XM249. It would be standardized in February 1982 by both the Army and Marines. Besides being belt-fed, it could accept an M16 magazine. Issue would be slow and production of the XM249E1 was suspended in 1985 owing to design problems; production resumed the next year. Many units did not receive the 5.56mm SAW until the 1990 Gulf War. It was type-classified the M249 SAW in 1994. Finally, the squad had a squad automatic weapon for the first time since the mid-1960s.

A splinter variant of the M16A1, developed by Rock Island Arsenal, Illinois, was adopted in 1978 as the M231 firing port weapon. It had 65 percent parts commonality with its parent, but was somewhat different internally. These were mounted in Bradley infantry fighting vehicle firing ports (two on each side and the rear; now only the two rear FPWs remain). They had no front sight, being aimed by bursts of 100 percent M196 tracers (different from the ammunition carried for the M16A2/A4 that Bradley infantrymen were armed with for dismounted operations), and fired full-automatic only in short bursts of 50–60rpm from an open bolt at 1,200rpm. Originally they were to be issued with a telescoping wire stock for emergency off-vehicle use, but the stocks were deleted. Handheld, it was too difficult to aim, other than just for spraying bullets, and suffered from severe muzzle climb, while the threaded mounting adapter overheated to burn unprotected hands, and its noise was above safe levels.

The 1980s saw an increase in production as the US armed forces were enlarged in light of the Soviet threat and M16s were offered to many friendly countries. In 1980 NATO adopted the Belgian-designed 5.56mm SS-109 ball and SS-110 tracer rounds (US M855 and M856). These heavier bullet rounds required a different rifling twist, 1-in-7in, to replace the M16A1's 1-in-12in twist. Other requirements were added to what was then known as the M16A1 PIP (Product Improvement Program): heavier barrel; improved handguard, butt and pistol grip; improved sights; the capability for left-handed shooters to fire safely; and other minor improvements. This formally became known as the M16A1E1 in 1981.

In October 1980 NATO standardized magazines for 5.56mm rifles (STANAG 4179). These are basically M16 magazines and may be made of metal, polyurethane, or other suitable materials. There is no specified

M231 firing port weapon characteristics

Caliber	5.56×45mm
Overall length	724mm (28.25in)
Barrel length	396mm (15.6in)
Weight without magazine	3.3kg (7.34lb)
Magazine	30-round curved
Cyclic rate	1,200rpm
Mode of fire	full-automatic only
Muzzle velocity	914m/s (2,998fps)
Effective range	300m (330yd)

Post-Vietnam M16/M4 weapons

Military designation	Used by	Colt model	Production
M16A2 rifle	Army, Marines	645	1984–96
M16A3 rifle	Navy	646	1996–97 & later
M16A4 rifle	Army, Marines	945	1996–present
Mk 12 Mod 0/1	Army, Navy	–	2000–c.2006
M4 carbine	All services	920	1987–present
M4A1 carbine	All services	921	1987–present

quality level. The STANAG is only a dimensional and magazine latch design requirement. They may be 20-, 30-, or 40-round box magazines or 90- or 100-round drum magazines. While the weapons in which they are used may differ greatly in design, the magazines are interchangeable. Over the years as new weapon designs have been fielded they have been adapted to accept the "STANAG magazine." Some weapons have been modified to take them, while some countries have not yet fielded weapons capable of accepting them. There are over 40 weapons (along with variants) that accept "NATO magazines."

THE M16A2, M16A3, AND M16A4 RIFLES

In 1978 the Army and Marines began discussions with regard to a product improved M16A1. In mid-1980 the Marines renewed the effort as the Army was procrastinating. Colt was still producing M16A1s through extensions on the 1967 contract. Many M16A1s were wearing out and numerous improvements had been proposed for a new model, especially since a new rifling twist was required to accommodate the new NATO ammunition. Colt experienced a slump with reduced orders, labor disputes, and lawsuits through the 1980s.

In November 1981, 50 M16A1E1s were delivered for testing, which was successful. It was type-classified in September 1982 and made Standard A by both the Army and the Marines in November 1983 as the "rifle, 5.56mm, M16A2." An evaluation test in February 1983 saw the M16A1E1 meeting 19 of its requirements, partially meeting five, and failing three. These issues were resolved prior to series production. The first M16A2s were issued to the Marine Marksmanship Training Unit in January 1984. There were complaints that the three-round burst mechanism caused inconsistent trigger pull on semi-automatic fire. In early 1984 the M16A2 Enhanced Rifle program was initiated and redesignated the M16A2E1. This variant had the "flat-top receiver" with the formerly integral carrying handle now being detachable. This allowed night vision and optical sights to be fitted to receiver-top tactical rails.

In early 1984 Diemaco (which became Colt Canada in 2005) in Kitchener, Ontario began production of their variants of the M16A2, the

C7 rifle and C8 carbine (Colt Models 711 and 725). They retained the full-automatic capability and M16A1-type rear sight and butt. They are used by Canada, Denmark, the Netherlands, and Norway. The later C7A1 and C7A2 (adjustable butt), and C8A1 carbine had optical sights and rails (before the US adopted Picatinny rails) replacing the carrying handle.

During 1985 the Army ordered M16A2E1s for testing, but had yet to purchase M16A2s for troop issue. Over 217,000 rifles were ordered by both services in 1985/86 and they began to be issued in the Army in late 1986.

FN Manufacturing Incorporated (FNMI) in Columbia, South Carolina, had been manufacturing the 7.62mm M240 machine gun since the early 1980s as the M60's replacement. In September 1988 the Army awarded a massive contract to FN to produce the M16A2 rifle. Colt strongly protested the award, but the protest was denied by the General Services Administration in January 1989. Colt continued to produce M16A1s for foreign military sales as well as the M203, and also spare parts as the M16A1 remained in service into the 2000s. In late 1989 Air Force and Coast Guard M16s and M16A1s began to be upgraded to M16A2 standards. More were converted periodically through 2000. The Army and Marines acquired new M16A2s rather than upgrading M16A1s. The upgrade kit consisted of an entirely new upper receiver (with barrel, round handguard, gas tube and sights), butt, pistol grip, and firing mechanism to allow burst fire. The only difference between new M16A2s and the upgrade kit-modified M16A1s was that the latter lacked the reinforced pivot pin and reinforced lower receiver extensions. The lower receiver was remarked by stamping, with AUTO changed to BURST and A1 to A2.

The M16A2 rifle was a distinct upgrade from the M16A1 incorporating many improvements, some developed by Colt in the 1970s. The barrel was

US Marines at Camp Lemonnier, Djibouti, the only US military base in Africa, conduct practice firing with an M4 carbine and M16A2 rifle, 2003. Note the detachable carrying handle on the M4 while the M16A2 has an integral carrying handle. (USMC)

provided with a 1-in-7in twist to accommodate the new ammunition and the portion of the barrel forward of the handguard was thicker. This proved necessary as M16A1 barrels were occasionally bent, ever so slightly, during parachute landings and other falls. It had the benefit of reducing overheating and improving accuracy. The "birdcage" flash suppressor was provided with five slots, with the bottom closed to reduce kicking up dust in the prone position. The new front sight was a square post and adjustable for elevation while the fully adjustable rear sight could be dialed for ranges between 300 and 800m. The round handguard had upper and lower pieces and both were interchangeable, and had removable improved heat shields. The smaller diameter better accommodated women's hands. The handguard's spring-loaded retaining ring was angled instead of straight making it easier to slip back for handguard removal/installation. The plunger of the forward assist was changed from oval to round. The pistol grip was better contoured and checkered for a more positive grip, and it had a closed bottom. The butt was 0.625in (16mm) longer and filled with ten times stronger DuPont fiberglass-filled thermoset polymers with a cleaning-gear compartment and improved butt plate with a trapdoor. An integral spent case deflector was behind the ejection port allowing safe left-hand firing.

A major change was in the selective fire capability. The selector was marked SAFE, SEMI, and BURST. (From the M16A2 onwards this was also marked on the receiver's right side with an arrow on that end of the selector lever pin to allow left-hand shooters to see the setting.) Burst fire allowed three-round bursts rather than unrestricted full-automatic fire. It had been found that some soldiers tended to fire too-long automatic bursts, wasting ammunition. Testing showed that the three-shot burst better conserved ammunition and improved accuracy. There was a design flaw, however. If the trigger was released before the three rounds cycled

Operation *Just Cause*, Panama 1989 (opposite)

During Operation *Just Cause* 1st Platoon, Fleet Antiterrorist Security Team (FAST) Company, Marine Security Force Battalion, Atlantic, helped clear Arraiján District around Howland Air Force Base outside of Panama City. The unit was trained and equipped as a SWAT-type unit and its skills were invaluable for clearing buildings. The M16A2 rifle began to be issued by the Marines in the mid-1980s and offered many improvements over the M16A1. Most Army infantry units in Panama also had the M16A2. This Marine's M16A2 (left) mounts a Leatherwood 3–9× Adjustable Ranging Telescope, the same as used on the 7.62mm M21 and other period sniper rifles. M16s, even with a scope, lacked the long-range accuracy, impact force, and penetration of the M21 owing to the 5.56mm round's light propellant and bullet.

FAST Marines also carried 9mm M9 pistols and what was often called the "M16 submachine gun" (right). The special-procurement Colt Model 635 had the appearance of an M16, but internally the 9mm weapon was very different – blowback-operated rather than having a direct impingement gas-operated system; it had a 10.5in barrel plus a large case deflector aft of the ejection port. It used a 32-round magazine based on the Uzi design and a fixed magazine adapter in the magazine well. FAST Marines used commercially made SWAT web gear and magazine pouches.

POR PANAMA:
¡LA VIDA
25 ANIVERSARIO
DE LOS
MARTIRES
DE EN

SHUMATE

M16A2, M16A3, and M16A4 rifle characteristics

Caliber	5.56×45mm
Overall length	1,006mm (39.62in)
Barrel length	508mm (20in)
Weight without magazine	3.5kg (7.78lb) (M16A2, M16A3); 4.11kg (9.08lb) (M16A4)
Magazine	30-round curved
Cyclic rate	700–900rpm (M16A2, M16A3); 800rpm (M16A4)
Mode of fire	semi- & three-round burst (M16A2, M16A4); semi- & full-auto (M16A3)
Muzzle velocity	945m/s (3,100fps)
Effective range	500m (550yd)

Members of the 5th Marines zero their new AN/PVQ-31A Rifle Combat Optics, the Trijicon Advanced Combat Optical Gunsight (ACOG), on M16A4 rifles aboard the USS *Essex* (LHD-2 amphibious assault ship). The Marine in the foreground has fully exposed RAS tactical rails on both sides, top, and bottom of his handguard. The Marine beyond him has a partial cover on his side handguard and a full-length one on the top. (USMC)

through it would interrupt the burst and would not reset. For example, if only two rounds were fired and the trigger released, then when the trigger was squeezed again it would fire only one round, not a three-round burst. The mechanism was also accused of affecting semi-automatic accuracy owing to erratic trigger-pull with as much as 6lb variance. Special operations forces preferred full-automatic owing to their requirements for close-range confined-space clearing and a break-contact drill known as the peel-back or "banana peel" (described on page 58). The M16A2 weighed 1.35lb more than the M16A1.

There were complaints too that the smaller (short-range) rear sight aperture was too small and the larger (long-range) aperture too large. Additionally, the two apertures were not on the same plane when changed,

causing the bullet impact point to change slightly. Most soldiers simply left the rear sight on the lowest range setting (300m) since few engagements occurred beyond this range, although longer ranges are frequently demanded in Afghanistan. Many feel that a shorter range setting should be available owing to typical engagement ranges.

Owing to special forces' preference for a full-automatic capability, the Navy sponsored the M16A2E3 rifle developed by Colt, which was identical to the M16A2, but replaced the three-round burst capability with full-automatic. The SEALs began to receive it in 1992. It was standardized in 1996 as the "rifle, 5.56mm, M16A3" for use by the SEALs, Seabees (construction engineers), and security forces (and is not to be confused with the Colt commercial M16A3, a "flat-top" M16A2). Only 7,480 FN-made M16A3s were initially procured by the Navy. M16A3s later replaced the M14 as shipboard rifles. The transition was completed in 2007 with only two M14s remaining aboard as line-throwing rifles. Additional M16A3 production has since been undertaken by both FN and Colt. (The M16A2E2 was a contender for the canceled Advanced Combat Rifle.) Colt went into bankruptcy in 1992 and after streamlining its operations emerged from bankruptcy in 1994.

The success of the "flat-top receiver" on the M4 and the introduction of a wide range of optical sights and related accessories led to the M16A2E4 rifle, developed by Colt in the early 1990s. It was type-classified as the "rifle, 5.56mm, M16A4" in 1996 by the Army. The Marines adopted it in 1998. The Army began issuing it in January 1999, soon followed by the Marines. They did not begin issuing M16A4s in large numbers until just prior to the 2003 Iraq invasion. It is produced by Colt and FN and weighs 1.3lb more than the M16A2 and 2.65lb more than the M16A1. The M16A4 was almost identical to the M16A2, but featured the "flat-top receiver" with a detachable carrying handle/rear sight. Fixed atop the receiver was a Picatinny rail allowing optical and night vision sights to be fitted. In 2009, a specification for the M16A4 was issued that removed the carrying handle – it would no longer be issued with the M16A4. A back-up rear iron sight (BUIS) could be attached to the rail in event of a failed or damaged optical sight. Troops were not necessarily issued BUISs, and some deployed troops have purchased them from commercial sources. In 2009 the Marines were considering a four- or six-position collapsible butt for the M16A4, but this project was dropped with wider issue of the M4.

The M16A4 was modified by replacing the standard handguard with the Knight Armament Corporation's (KAC) M5 Rail Adapter System (RAS) to become the M16A4 Modular Weapon System (MWS) in

A typical sight picture of optical sights now routinely used on M16/M4s. It provides a red dot in the sight, replacing the rear iron ring sight, which is aligned with the front sight. (C. J. Harper)

41

The Picatinny rail

The idea of providing mounting rails on weapons to accommodate optical and night vision sights and other accessories originated with Reed Knight, Jr, president of Knight Armament Corporation (KAC), when he saw special forces troops during the 1989 Panama intervention with small flashlights taped to their weapons. There had to be a better way to mount such devices. KAC developed two systems, the Rail Interface System (RIS) and Rail Adapter System (RAS). The first systems were envisioned as mounting only optical and night vision sights and the rails were fitted atop weapons. The idea of the long rail mount was to allow any kind of sight to be fitted through the use of a standard integral mount. In the past telescopes and night vision sights had often had different mounts and special adapters had had to be provided to mate them to different weapons. The mounts were track-like brackets provided with two, four, six, and eleven ribs allowing sights and accessories to be fitted in any position as desired by the shooter. On the M4/M4A1 and M16A4 they were fitted on the top, sides, and bottom of the handguard. Slip-on polymer covers were available to slide over unused rails to provide a better grip and protect against inducted firing heat. The challenges included how to solidly mount the rail on the weapon to prevent play, so that sights mounted on the rails would not lose their zero within 10,000 rounds, and so that overheated barrels would not twist them. The XM4 for M4 and XM5 for M16A4 were developed in 1997 based on the KAC RAS. M4s and M16A4s fitted with the rails are referred to as the Modular Weapon System (MWS). The adapter rail systems were classified as Standard A in April 1998 and first issued in October.

ABOVE A close-up of a US Air Force security policeman's M4 carbine at Davis-Monthan Air Force Base, 2008. His M4 mounts RAS tactical rails with an ECOS-N M68 close-combat optical sight and an AN/PEQ-2 infrared illuminator. (USAF)

Final development and testing was undertaken at Picatinny Arsenal, New Jersey (pronounced "Pick uh TIN nee") resulting in their being known as "Picatinny rails"; they are also referred to as "MIL-STD-1913 tactical rails" (after the military specification number) or "STANAG 2324 rails" (after the NATO standardization agreement). A wide variety of sights and accessories can be fitted to Picatinny rails including telescopes, reflex sights such as the ECOS, laser pointers/illuminators, visible lasers, flashlights, backup iron sight, vertical handgrips, bipods, M203/M320 grenade launchers, and M26 breaching shotguns.

1997. This was a spinoff from the M4 program. The MWS handguard has Picatinny tactical rails on the top, bottom, and sides to allow sights, flashlights, hand grips, 40mm grenade launchers, and other accessories to be solidly fitted. There were no differences between the dimensions of the M16A2 rifle and the M16A4 MWS rifle.

THE M4 AND M4A1 CARBINES

In the early 1980s interest was revived in the idea of a short version of the M16. In September 1984 the M16A2 carbine program was established and, following the sequence of the .30cal M1, M2, and M3 carbines of the 1940s and 1950s, was designated the XM4. The new Colt-developed weapon would be designated a carbine with a 14.5in barrel as opposed to the XM177E2 submachine gun with an 11.5in barrel. In the middle of 1985 XM4 carbines were ordered for testing, which continued into the next year. The design retained the M16A2's three-round burst capability.

M4 and M4A1 carbine characteristics

Caliber	5.56×45mm
Overall length (extracted)	838mm (33in)
Overall length (retracted)	756mm (29.75in)
Barrel length	368mm (14.5in)
Weight without magazine	2.88kg (6.36lb)
Magazine	30-round curved
Cyclic rate	700–950rpm
Mode of fire	semi- & 3-round burst (M4); semi- & full-auto (M4A1)
Muzzle velocity	884m/s (2,900fps)
Effective range	450m (490yd)

The Army classified the XM4 as the "carbine, 5.56mm, M4" on January 30, 1987, but it was not issued until April 1989. In April 1987 the Marines standardized the M4, but Congress rejected its inclusion in the budget. The project was inactive until the late 1990s. Special forces wanted a full-automatic capability so a second version was developed as the M4E1. It became the M4A1. All M4s and M4A1s were made by Colt, but the Army acquired the rights and technical data package for the M4 from Colt, making it possible to contract other producers under special circumstances, but the M4 Amendment again restricted its production to Colt.

The Army originally intended for the M4 to replace many M9 pistols and certain M16s in combat units among officers, weapons crewmen, radio operators, etc. It would also finally replace M3A1 grease guns as on-vehicle equipment aboard tanks. Special forces units were also interested in it as a close-quarter battle carbine to replace MP5s and other

An M4A1 carbine with RAS tactical rails, fitted with an ECOS-N M68 close-combat optical sight with an AN/PAQ-4 infrared aiming light attached atop it, backup iron sight, and a combination fore grip and bipod. The small bipod legs can be retracted into the fore grip. It also is fitted with the Sloping Cheekweld Buttstock developed by Naval Weapons Center, Crane Division. (US Army)

weapons. The Marines planned to assign M4s to officers below colonel, senior NCOs, small-unit leaders, and medical corpsmen. Reconnaissance units were still using the M3A1, but these were replaced by H&K 9mm MP5-N submachine guns after the Congressional rejection of the M4.

The Marines conducted tests throughout 2002 to determine if the M16A4 or the M4A1 would better serve as an infantry weapon. The Marines initially decided that the M16A4 would arm infantrymen and the M4A1 would equip reconnaissance and special units. The Army began arming Stryker infantry units (eight-wheel infantry carriers), light infantry, airborne, air assault, and Rangers with M4s in about 1999. Other troops retained the M16A2s and A4s. In late 2002 the Air Force began replacing its M16s, M16A2s, and GAU-5 (XM177) weapons with M4s fitted with M68 optical sights. By 2005 infantry units were being equipped solely with the M4, especially those deploying to Iraq and Afghanistan.

The XM4 was to be compatible with the new M855 ammunition as well as the older M193. It was to have the M16A2's upper receiver, but with a 14.5in barrel, and would retain the three-round burst capability. Some 75 percent of the parts are compatible with the M16A1/A2. It had

As can be seen the M4 carbine (bottom) with a 14.5in barrel is much more than a simple update of the Vietnam-era XM177E2 submachine gun (top) with an 11.5in barrel. This is a commercial/law enforcement version of the M4 with numerous after-market accessories and fittings plus an ACOG sight. (Trey Moore collection)

to be able to mount an M203 grenade launcher. The M203A1 for the M4 was designed in 1997. Both the M4 and M4A1 had flat-top rail receivers and detachable carrying handles. The XM4 and the first lot of M4s had fixed carrying handles, though.

To accommodate the detachable carrying handle the front sight post had to be heightened. The weapon also had an extended feed ramp. This meant the carbines' zeroing method was different to the M16A2/A4's and this occasionally resulted in improper zeroing using the M16A2/A4 method. A telescoping butt stock was provided with four positions: closed, half open, three-quarters open, and fully open. Some units received an improved butt developed by Naval Weapons Center, Crane Division, known as the Sloping Cheekweld Buttstock, and it was issued in some SOPMOD kits. Other units have purchased various commercially made

SOPMOD M4A1 Block 1 accessory kit

Development of the Special Operations Peculiar Modification kit began in 1989 to provide special forces units with a wide range of accessories and devices to tailor M4A1 carbines for mission and situational requirements. It was adopted in 1993 and each set supported four M4A1s. Many of the components are non-developmental and commercial off-the-shelf items. As improved items are developed many units purchase these and replace lost or damaged items or substitute them with new devices. Items are often cannibalized between kits. The original SOPMOD Block I kit included the following items:

4× KAC rail interface system forearms
4× KAC vertical foregrips
4× KAC backup iron sights
4× Trijicon TA01NSN 4×32 advanced combat optical gunsights (ACOG)
4× ECOS-N M68 close-combat optical sights
4× Tactical Ordnance & Equipment improved combat slings
4× PRI bracket mount for AN/PVS-14 night vision sights
4× Insight Technology AN/PEQ-2 infrared target pointer/illuminator/aiming lasers
2× Insight Technology visible Bright Light II illuminators
2× Trijicon RX01M4A1 reflex sights
2× KAC quick-detach sound suppressors
1× KAC quick-attach M203 grenade launcher mount
1× quick-attach M203 leaf sight
1× shortened (9in) M203 grenade launcher
1× Insight Technology AN/PEQ-5 visible laser
1× AN/PVS-17A mini-night vision sight
1× AN/PSQ-18A M203 day/night sight
1× carrying/storage case for kit

SOPMOD Block II kit is under development and might include a 12-gauge M26 modular accessory shotgun system (MASS) and 40mm M320 grenade launcher. A goal is to provide items requiring either no batteries or standard batteries only. SOPMOD Block III will have accessories compatible with the M4A1 carbine and the FN 5.56mm Mk 16 Mod 0 Light (SCAR-L) and the 7.62mm Mk 17 Mod 0 Heavy (SCAR-H) special forces combat assault rifles.

butts. The front sling swivel was on the left side of the front sight, with a bayonet lug below, and the rear swivel was on the upper end of the butt with an alternate slot below the recoil buffer tube. The butt's latch lever was on the underside of the butt's forward end. The short handguard was prone to overheating so a two-layer heat shield was provided. The M4E2 (Colt Model 925) had the M4 rail system fitted and this was incorporated into later production M4A1s.

Complaints from Iraq, and to a lesser extent Afghanistan, called for a more compact weapon to improve maneuverability in buildings, on rough terrain, and for mounted troops (in Bradleys, Strykers, Humvees, and Mine Resistant Ambush Protected (MRAP) vehicles) as well as in helicopters and watercraft; the compact size would also be useful in parachute operations. Some troops were picking up folding-stock AK-47s as a more convenient weapon and to achieve better penetration. The desire for a more compact weapon, plus its admittedly "sexier" look, led to the widespread use of the M4 in lieu of the M16A4 in combat units. The value of compactness outweighed concerns about the M4's shorter barrel reducing range, penetration, velocity, and killing power. The shorter gas tube resulted in harder wear on parts and the muzzle blast was louder. In 1997 the Army announced that it would gradually replace the M16A2 with M4 "flat-top" carbines in combat units. In late 2000 the Marines began exercises to test the suitability of the M4 being issued Corps-wide. From 2000 some special forces units were provided with some heavy barrels as replacements for M4A1 light barrels. Major fielding of the M16A4 and M4 with tactical rails commenced in 2001. Tellingly, soldiers now refer to the M16-series rifles as "muskets," denoting how "ancient" they are compared to the M4.

Mk 12 SPECIAL PURPOSE RIFLE

The special purpose rifle (SPR) concept began to be developed in 2000 having been proposed by Mark Westrom at Rock Island Arsenal (later ArmaLite president). While recognizing that it would not be a true sniper rifle, special forces units desired a light and compact designated-marksman rifle that would offer more range and precision fire than the M4A1, yet be shorter than the M16A2/4. The developmental history of the Mk 12 is foggy with work done on various developmental variants by Rock Island and Naval Weapons Center, Crane along with civilian corporation contributions. It is an outgrowth of the SEALs' Recon Rifle project. The original SPR concept called for it to consist only of the specially modified upper receiver and barrel; the idea was for the SPR upper receiver and barrel to be mated to any M16A1/A2 or M4A1 lower receiver. At some point it was decided to provide a complete system with a lower receiver. The uppers were often made by Diemaco/Colt Canada and ArmaLite. Lower receivers were fitted with a KAC two-stage trigger for improved trigger pull allowing match-quality semi-automatic fire as well as the ability to lay down full-automatic suppression in an emergency. Later Mk

The Mk 12 Mod 1 special purpose rifle, the Mod 1 being developed by Naval Weapons Center, Crane Division. The Mod 0 was developed by Rock Island Arsenal. These weapons, intended to provide more accurate and longer-ranged fire than M4 carbines, mostly use M4 "flat-top" receivers with a match-grade 18in barrel and an M16A1 lower receiver modified with a two-stage trigger for improved trigger pull. It is fitted with a Crane Sloping Cheekweld Buttstock. The telescope is a 3.5–10× Leupold LR M3, one of several types of scope available. (US Navy)

12s used M4 "flat-top" receivers and M16A1 lowers. The 18in match-grade barrels were stainless steel with a 1-in-7in twist and a special flash suppressor. A variety of special handguards were found with different tactical rail configurations and a small forward-folding, adjustable bipod on the forward end. Handguards were the free-floating type that did not come into direct contact with the barrel, to reduce heat effects, vibrations, and pressure. The familiar triangular M16 front sight frame was replaced by a variety of flip-up sights. Common telescopes mounted on long receiver-top rails included the 3.5–10× Leupold LR M3, 2.5–9× TS-30, and 3–9× TS-30A2, and 2.5–10× Nightforce NXS. The weapon used Mk 262 match ammunition with a heavier bullet than standard ball rounds. The Mk 12 is issued with 20-round magazines to better accommodate prone firing. The Mk 12 Mod 0 is used by Army Special Forces and the Mod 1 by SEALs and Army Rangers. Reports indicate that many users preferred the Mod 0 owing to better ergonomics, but many SEALs were disappointed with the SPR, preferring a 16in barrel carbine rather than a militarized match rifle.

Mk 12 Mod 0/1 special purpose rifle characteristics

Caliber	5.56×45mm
Overall length	957mm (37.5in)
Barrel length	457mm (18in)
Weight without magazine*	4.08kg (9lb)
Magazine	20-round straight
Cyclic rate	700–950rpm
Mode of fire	semi- & full-auto
Muzzle velocity	930m/s (3,050fps)
Effective range	550m (600yd)

*Weight varies with specific configuration.

ABOVE The Mk 12 Mod 1. (US Navy)

M16/M4 ACCESSORIES

Over the years a wide range of accessories, add-ons, and specialized sights have been made available for the M16/M4. Space does not allow a detailed examination of the many accessories, but a short overview is provided here.

The M1 sling was an olive drab nylon web sling with metal hardware. Later a lighter-weight black sling with metal hardware was issued with the M16A2. Since the late 1990s a number of styles of black tactical or assault slings have been available with nylon plastic fittings. These three-point slings allow the rifle to be suspended from the shoulder or around the neck and the weapon carried in a ready mode.

The Vietnam-era XM3 bipod was a non-folding cloth-pin type that clipped onto the barrel below the front sight and was non-adjustable for height. It was carried in a canvas or nylon case with a zippered pocket on the side for cleaning gear. It was envisioned that every man would be issued one, but it saw little use.

The Vietnam-era cleaning kit was also issued in a nylon pouch, usually carried inside the rucksack, containing: sectionalized cleaning rod, slotted patch tip, chamber and bore brushes, 2oz and 4oz bottles of LSA (lubricant, small arms); pipe cleaners for cleaning the gas tube, gas key and other hard-to-reach places; and cleaning patches (7.62mm patches had to be cut into quarters; smaller patches were later issued). Many soldiers provided themselves with a toothbrush and shaving brush for effective cleaning. An issue toothbrush-like brush was soon provided with a regular brush head on one end and a small one on the other. From 1969 the M16A1 and later full-stock M16s had a butt trap for a cleaning kit. This was contained in an elongated triangular-shaped cloth envelope. The early M11 cleaning rods were three-piece with a knuckled handle end. The later cleaning rod was four-piece with a folding "T" handle (often called five-piece including the patch-holder tip). A new lubricant, CLP (cleaner, lubricant, preservative), was introduced in the mid-1980s. In Vietnam some men stuffed cleaning

An M16A1 rifle mounting a Colt/Realist 3× telescope. Almost 400 were sent to Vietnam in March 1967 and used by specialist marksmen. It by no means turned the M16 into a sniper rifle. The carrying handle proved to be an inadequate mount for telescopes. (Trey Moore collection)

patches or a small rag into the hollow pistol grip, holding them in place with duct tape. LSA bottles were sometimes inserted in helmet camouflage bands.

The 6.5in-blade double-edged M7 bayonet and M8A1 fiberglass scabbard were adopted in 1964 and based on the M14 rifle's M6, itself derived from the M2 carbine's bayonet. The M9 multipurpose bayonet system and nylon M10 scabbard were adopted in 1984 by the Army and Marines. Issue began in 1987, but it was years before it replaced the M7, which still remains in use in training units. It was designed to provide a better utility and fighting knife, as well as serve as a wire-cutter via a hole in the blade mating with a lug on the scabbard. It also had a serrated upper blade allowing it to saw wood and cut through aluminum aircraft fuselages. The 7in-blade M9 could be used on M16s and M4s. In 2003 the Marines began issuing the USMC multipurpose bayonet with a thermoplastic scabbard. It was based on the K-Bar fighting knife and had no wire-cutting ability. It had only a short serrated edge on the 8in blade's lower edge forward of the guard.

Several types of silencers or sound suppressors have been used on the M16/M4. The Human Engineering Laboratory (HEL) M4 and SIONICS MAW-556 and E4A were three of many models used in Vietnam along with test models. More recently a number of commercially purchased suppressors have been used. The current standard device is the KAC quick-detachable suppressor offering a 25-decibel sound reduction and 3,000-round life.

The rifleman's assault weapon (RAW) was developed in the mid-1970s and saw limited use by the Marines in the 1990s. This was a disposable launcher device that attached to the M16A1/A2's bayonet lug. When the rifle was fired with a ball round, gas was bled off and initiated the RAW's launch. It projected a rocket-propelled, spin-stabilized 140mm 2.2lb spherical high-explosive projectile up to 300m to blast a 14in-diameter hole through 8in of reinforced concrete.

The 12-gauge M26 modular accessory shotgun system (MASS) was introduced in 2005 with initial issue in 2008 and full issue in 2011. This is a straight-pull, bolt-action shotgun with a five-round magazine.

The 12-gauge M26 modular accessory shotgun system can be mounted under an M4, as here, or an M16-series rifle. It is a straight-pull bolt-action breaching shotgun with a five-round magazine. It is fitted with an ECOS-N M68 close-combat optical sight with an AN/PAQ-4 infrared aiming light attached atop it. (US Army)

The 12-gauge M26 modular accessory shotgun system mounted on an M4 carbine (with an ACOG sight) was first issued in 2008. This particular test version has a longer than standard barrel – the standard barrel does not extend beyond the M4's muzzle. (US Army)

An M16A1 rifle with a MILES (Multiple Integrated Laser Engagement System) fitted on the barrel along with a red M15A2 blank firing adapter. These are used during force-on-force training exercises. The sound of a blank firing fires an eye-safe laser. If an opposing soldier is "hit" it is detected by the small black dome-shaped laser receivers worn on his helmet and torso harness. This activates a buzzer and a small flashing light on his left shoulder. The buzzer and light can only be turned off by an accompanying observer/controller (umpire). (Texas Military Forces Museum)

It mounts under an M16/M4 and can fire 00 buckshot, breaching rounds, tear gas, and non-lethal loads. The MASS can also be fitted with a standalone M4-style collapsible butt and pistol grip. It weights 2lb 11oz in the under-barrel mode and 4lb 3oz as a standalone.

In 2007 the close-quarters battle kit was introduced providing units with accessories to enhance the M16/M4 for short-range action, especially in urban areas. It includes: an improved cleaning kit, tactical sling, multiple magazine holder, bottom-mounted forward rail bracket, bipod/forward grip, and squad designated marksman bipod.

It was several years after the standardization of the XM16E1 before blank ammunition and adapters were available. The M15A1/A2 blank firing attachments (BFA, aka blank adapters) for the M16-series rifles are painted red while the M23 for the M4 is yellow. BFAs are designed so that if ball ammunition is accidently fired it will knock the adapter off without weapon damage or injury to the firer (the author has seen this occur). "Hollywood" blank adapters used in movies/TV and by re-enactors are inserts fitted in the muzzle with the flash suppressor reinstalled. Plastic muzzle caps (black or red) keep water, dust, and foreign matter out of the barrel. They can be safely shot through.

The M2 practice bolt and carrier replaces the standard assembly to allow the use of M862 short-range training ammunition on 25m alternate qualification ranges. This is a small plastic bullet with the same dispersion as ball ammunition at short ranges. The M261 .22 Long Rifle rimfire conversion kit provides a special bolt carrier assembly and 25-round magazine for use on indoor ranges. The black nylon plastic cartridge case deflector assembly could be fitted on the right side of the M16A1 to allow left-handed shooters to fire safely.

AMMUNITION

The M16 is chambered for a unique cartridge, which contributed more to the weapon's controversy than the weapon itself. The 5.56×45mm was much influenced by the .222 Remington. This was introduced in 1950 as a varmint/small game cartridge for the new Remington Model 722 bolt-action rifle. The cartridge was similar in class to the obsolete .219 Zipper, but was a modern rimless, steep-shoulder design for bolt-action rifles. It proved quite popular with varmint hunters and benchrest competitive shooters. Intended to fill the performance gap between the old .218 Bee and .220 Swift, the .222 was basically a scaled-down .30-06. It was available in soft-point and hollow-point bullets.

In the late 1950s several manufacturers were developing small-caliber cartridges based on the .222 Remington for the Small-Caliber High-Velocity Rifle program. The goal was to create a small high-velocity .22cal cartridge that maintained a supersonic velocity at 500 yards (1,080fps at sea level). This could not be achieved by the popular .222 Remington. A longer case was necessary to contain additional propellant. Remington and Springfield Armory developed the .224 Springfield. The Springfield project was dropped, but in 1958 the cartridge was released commercially as the .222 Remington Magnum. At the same time Winchester developed what was known as the .224 E1 and E2 Winchester rounds, but it too dropped out of the project.

Remington and ArmaLite teamed up to develop a round for the weapon that would become the M16 in 1957. Robert Hutton, a *Guns & Ammo* magazine editor, was responsible for the round's design and it was introduced as the .222 Remington Special. What became known as the .223 Remington had a 1.76in-long case while the .222 was 1.7in long. Other case dimensions were identical or similar. It was designed as a supplementary military cartridge specifically for the AR-15 rifle and initially had a 55-grain full-metal-jacket bullet. The actual bullet caliber of both the .222 and .223 is .224cal (5.689mm). In 1962 Remington introduced its Model 700 bolt-action rifle in a wide range of calibers and added the .223 Remington in 1964. With its higher velocity and use by the military, the .223 soon replaced the .222 in the varmint and competitive shooting fields.

Owing to NATO standardization requirements, the military designated the new round the 5.56mm when adopting it in 1963. From 1980, when it was adopted by NATO, it became known as the 5.56mm NATO. The media often stated that the Army was adopting a ".22cal" cartridge, leading those unfamiliar with weapons to think of the .22 Long Rifle rimfire and tin can plinking.

A comparison of cartridges. For scale, the US 1 cent (penny) is 19.05mm (0.750in) and the 10 Euro cent 19.75mm (0.777in).

Left to right: 7.62×51mm NATO (M14, FAL, G3); .30 Carbine; 5.56×45mm NATO (M16/M4); 6.8mm SPC (replacement contender for 5.56mm); 7.62×39mm (Soviet/Russian AK-47); 5.45×49mm (Soviet/Russian AK-74); and 9×19mm Parabellum/NATO (widely used in pistols and submachine guns). (Author's collection)

Chamber dimensions between military 5.56mm and commercial .223 rounds are slightly different. The MIL-SPEC chamber has a longer "leade," the distance between the cartridge mouth and the point where rifling engages the bullet. Commercial ammunition can be fired in military weapons, but where military ammunition is fired in commercial weapons slightly higher chamber pressures may develop leading to excessive wear and stress. There have been no reports of weapon damage or injury.

The idea for the .22cal high-velocity light rifle round originated in 1953 when M2 carbines were modified with .22cal barrels and a small muzzle brake. They used a .222 Remington case shortened to 1.32in with a 41-grain bullet. The tests confirmed that the carbine was an under-performing weapon and that the .22 Carbine performed well enough when compared to the .30 Carbine, but had poorer striking energy. The conclusion was that the .22cal round had potential as a replacement for .45cal submachine guns. It was not considered for use as the standard rifle round, as the 7.62×51mm was near to being accepted as the new rifle and machine-gun round for not only the USA, but NATO.

The first ball round was the M193 with a 55-grain lead-cored bullet. Besides the previously discussed early ball powder problem, the bullet was simply too light to be truly effective. It was barely twice the weight of the .22 Long Rifle lead bullet. The 7.62×51mm NATO M80 ball had a 150-grain bullet and the Soviet 7.62×39mm used in the AK-47 had a 125-grain steel-cored bullet. The 5.56mm's light bullet and high velocity gave an impressive performance, but there were some problems that were often discounted. A light bullet traveling at a high speed is easily deflected by vegetation and lacks penetration ability. Such a bullet might inflict horrible wounds, but if it is deflected, shattered, or deformed when hitting typical cover materials such as brick walls, logs, board fences, building walls and floors, sandbags, foxhole earth parapets, and so on, it is of little use. Many were enamored of early AR-15 demonstrations in which a shooter emptied

5.56×45mm ammunition

Cartridge	Identification	Remarks
Ball, MLU-26/P	plain tip	Early USAF
Ball, M193	plain tip	
Ball, M855	green tip	
Ball, M885A1	steel tip	
Special ball, Mk 262 Mod 0/1		
Enhanced ball, Mk 318 Mod 0		aka SOST
Armor-piercing, M995	black tip	
Tracer, M193	red tip	
Tracer, M856	red tip*	
Dim tracer, XM996	dark violet tip†	
Short-range training, M862	light blue plastic bullet	
Grenade launcher, M195	red rosette crimp	
Airfoil munition launcher, M755	yellow rosette crimp	M234 launcher
Blank, M200	dark violet rosette crimp	
High pressure test, M197	silvered case	Should not be fired in service weapons
Dummy, M199	longitudinal flutes	
Dummy, M232	blackened case	

* Orange tip if linked for SAW.
† Can be observed only by night vision devices.

Remarks

Ammunition designated below M200 is first generation for 1-in-12in twist rifling while those above M200 are NATO standard for 1-in-7in twist and in current use.

RIGHT Vietnam-era cartons each holding seven 20-round M16A1 magazines, Federal Stock Number 1005-056-2237. The minimal basic load was considered nine magazines, but in combat soldiers frequently carried up to 20 or more. (Trey Moore collection)

a magazine at short range to literally chew through a cinder block. It required some 35 rounds to shoot a loophole-sized hole through a 12in sand-filled cinder block, while it takes 18 to do the same with 7.62mm. There were reports, too, of horrendous wounds, alongside tales of multiple hits failing to stop an enemy.

NATO standardized the FN-designed SS109 ball and L110 tracer in October 1980 (STANAG 4172). Member countries adapted the designs to their own production requirements and the US designated them M855 and M856, respectively. These rounds were designed to achieve better penetration through helmets and body armor. This green-tipped ball round had a "heavier" 62-grain bullet (7 grains heavier than the M193), but had a steel core to slightly improve penetration. Its lower velocity improved long-range performance. The M855 proved more destructive to tissue at ranges over 45m from the M4 and at over 120m with the M16. There were still numerous complaints of inadequate incapacitation after multiple hits. The bullet was more stable and often failed to yaw or fragment when hitting a limb or lightly built individual, instead passing through the target before yawing occurred. The M855A1 enhanced performance round introduced in mid-2010 was a two-piece 62-grain bullet. The rear half of the bullet core was a bismuth-tin alloy slug and the front half a hardened steel "stacked cone" penetrator with its tip exposed.

The black-tipped M995 armor-piercing was introduced in 2001. The tungsten penetrator was capable of piercing a 3mm steel helmet at 600m and up to 0.5in hardened steel at 100m at zero degrees impact, making it suitable for urban targets and light armored vehicles.

In search of a better-performing round, special forces adopted the Mk 262 Mod 1 and 2 77-grain long-range special ball in 2002. The Mod 2 bullet added a cannelure for more effective case crimping. Originally designed for the Mk 12 special purpose rifle, it began to be used by most special forces units. It offered a heavier bullet to improve range, but also fragmented more effectively. This was a high-quality match-grade bullet with an open tip[6] optimized for the M4A1. The round did sacrifice penetration as it lacked a steel core. It was also costly.

Poncho-clad infantry trainees load 20-round magazines using 10-round charging clips (aka "stripper clips") with loading adapters or guides (aka "spoons"). The red helmets were worn by range support personnel – this duty rotated between trainees. (Ft Polk Museum)

A rifleman collecting spent brass during target practice. A 20× M49 spotting telescope sits to his left. The three-magazine ALICE magazine pouch can be seen on his right hip. (Texas Military Forces Museum)

The Mk 318 Mod 0 enhanced ball appeared in early 2009 and was developed by the US Special Operations Command, mainly for the Mk 16 Mod 0 special forces combat assault rifle-light (SCAR-L), which required a more accurate bullet for the close-quarter battle version with its 13.8in barrel. It was also effective in the M16 and M4. It used a 62-grain open-tip match bullet also known as the Special Operations Science and Technology (SOST) round. It had a lead core forward and the rear half of the bullet was solid copper to serve as a penetrator. It was designed to be "barrier blind," meaning that it stayed on trajectory better than M855 rounds after penetrating windshields, car doors, and other light materials. In 2010 the Marines adopted the Mk 318 as standard rather than use the Army's new M855A1.

In 2001 members of the 5th Special Forces Group and the Army Marksmanship Unit developed the 6.8mm Special Purpose Cartridge (SPC)[7] for use in modified M4A1 and Mk12 SPRs. The 43mm-long case was slightly shorter than the 5.56mm's, but the 115-grain .277cal bullet was longer, making the two rounds the same length and the 6.8mm case larger in diameter. This proved to be a very accurate and potent cartridge, bridging the gap between the 5.56mm and 7.62mm. New upper receivers, barrels, and modified bolts could be fitted to M4A1 and Mk 12 lower receivers. It required special 25-round magazines, but they fit the existing magazine well. From 2003 6.8mm weapons were used in Afghanistan on a limited basis, but it was deemed impractical to change to a new caliber and magazines.

[6] Open-tip bullets are *not* hollow-points. The tiny indentation on the tip does not pierce the jacket or extend into the core. The open-tip helps stabilize the bullet

[7] Sometimes called the 6.8mm Remington SPC as the cartridge is based on the .30 Remington case introduced in 1906, a rimless version of the .30-30 Winchester for the Remington Model 8 self-loading rifle

USE
Vietnam, Iraq, and beyond

FIRING THE M16

Firing the M16 is straightforward and simple. Magazines are typically loaded one or two rounds fewer than their rated capacity. The magazine's back edge can be tapped on a helmet, rifle butt, or boot heel to set the cartridges, preventing bullet tips from digging into the magazine's front edge. With the selector lever set on Safe, the user inserts the magazine into the well until the catch clicks, slaps the bottom, and tugs down on it to ensure the catch holds. To load the weapon the charging handle is pulled rearward and released to chamber a round as the bolt runs forward. If time permits, the charging handle can be pulled slightly to the rear, enough to confirm that a round is in the chamber. The user should not pull it too far back or the round may be ejected or result in a double-feed. The forward assist device is tapped with the heel of the hand ensuring positive locking and the ejection port cover is closed if the weapon is not to be fired immediately.

To fire, the selector lever on the left side is moved to the Semi-Auto, Burst or Full-Auto position as appropriate. It is interesting to note that the M16/M4 selector settings go from Safe to Semi-Auto then to Burst or Full-Auto, emphasizing that semi-automatic is the preferred mode. The AK-47 selector, on the other hand, was moved from Safe to Full-Auto to Semi-Auto, demonstrating the Soviet/Russian preference for massed full-automatic fire.

The butt is pulled firmly into the shoulder and because of the weapon's high line of sight, it is frequently set high on the pit of the shoulder or even on the collarbone. The cheek is placed firmly against the stock ensuring a firm "weld." The right hand holds the pistol grip firmly and the left hand grips the handguard where it is most comfortable. Often now a detachable forward grip or grip/bipod is attached to a tactical rail under the handguard. Some grip the magazine and well; while this is considered acceptable, it is often discouraged as it can put unnecessary pressure on the magazine. There are so many different types of sights that the sight picture is not discussed here (the standard iron sights are assumed). After the range has been set, the front post sight is centered on the target and aligned with and centered in the rear peep sight. A complaint with iron sights is that they are high, 2.5in over the bore. This creates a parallax (difference in sight and bore alignment) within 15–20m, requiring the shooter to aim a bit higher to hit a precise point. Of course in combat conditions on a man-sized target this is a moot point. A more serious complaint is that the shortest range setting is 300m and most combat shooting takes place at much closer ranges.

With the target in the sight the trigger is squeezed gently, not jerked, even on full-automatic. The shot should come as a "surprise." The trigger pull is 7.5lb, but there can be a slight variance. Single shots or full-automatic bursts are repeated as necessary. Recoil is very light. Even placing the butt on the chin and firing provides a "gentle" recoil. Some instructors have emphasized this by firing it with the butt in their crotch. The noise and muzzle blast levels are acceptable, although it is increased for "shorty M16s," for example the XM177 or the M4.

When the magazine is empty the bolt will remain open. The magazine is ejected and replaced and the bolt release lever on the right side is pressed to allow it to run forward to chamber a round. The forward assist is slapped and the weapon is ready to fire.

In the event of a stoppage a standard immediate action drill is applied to reduce the stoppage. The key word S P O R T S helps the firer remember the steps in order:

1. *Slap* gently upward on the magazine to ensure that it is fully seated, and that the magazine follower is not jammed.
2. *Pull* the charging handle fully to the rear.
3. *Observe* for the ejection of a live round or expended cartridge. (If the weapon fails to eject a cartridge, perform remedial action.)
4. *Release* the charging handle (do not ride it forward).
5. *Tap* the forward assist assembly to ensure bolt closure.
6. *Squeeze* the trigger and try to fire the rifle.

A US Navy Mobile Riverine Force sailor fires an early production XM16E1 into riverbank foliage where VC movement was spotted, Mekong Delta, 1967. Note the lack of a forward assist device. Prior to 1967 riverine assault and support craft of the MRF were armed with Mk 1 Mod 2 rifles – M1 Garands converted to 7.62mm NATO. (Bettmann/Corbis)

OPPOSITE

1. This recreation demonstrates the ease with which an M16A1 rifle could be carried simply by placing the magazine between an ammunition pouch and a canteen carrier – or between two ammunition pouches – and holding it in place by the natural hang of the right arm. It could be brought to the firing position in a second. For this reason many men removed the sling altogether. Note the magazine loading guide under the helmet band and the issue double-ended cleaning "toothbrush" inserted in a hole in the camouflage cover.

2. This recreation shows the XM3 "cloth-pin" bipod clipped on to the M16A1. In theory every rifleman was to be issued a bipod, which was carried in a canvas or nylon case with cleaning gear (there was no butt trap for cleaning gear on early-production M16A1s and earlier models). In practice very few used the cumbersome bipods. They were extremely prone to snagging in brush.

3. This demonstrates the actions taken by a rifleman with an expended case jammed in the chamber. He had to pull out the upper-receiver rear retaining pin (which remained attached), open the receiver, pull back the operating handle, remove it and the bolt carrier, insert a cleaning rod (which had to be screwed together), punch out the stuck case, and reassemble the weapon. The T-shaped operating handle can be seen under the magazine and the bolt carrier is beside the LSA bottle. It was very easy to lose the operating handle. The XM3 bipod and cleaning gear case can be seen above the magazine. (Courtesy of David Trentham)

Remedial action is performed to determine a stoppage's cause and to try to clear the stoppage once it has been identified. The user first tries to place the weapon on Safe, remove the magazine, and lock the bolt to the rear. Then the weapon may be disassembled and examined to determine the malfunction. These include failure to: feed, chamber, or lock; fire the cartridge; extract; or eject.

To clear the weapon it is kept on Safe, the magazine is ejected, the charging handle is pulled to the rear to eject the chambered round (which is reinserted in the magazine), the ejection port cover is closed, and it is verified that the weapon is on Safe.

The XM16E1/M16A1 had a distinctly flimsy feel enhanced by the feel of the buffer spring when firing. This applies to any extremely light weapon. The M16A2 and subsequent models have a somewhat more solid feel to them, but nothing approaching earlier battle rifles like the M1, M14, FAL, etc. The black rifle's light weight and apparent flimsiness made it extremely poor for close combat using either the rifle butt or bayonet.

There are pros and cons in regards to full-automatic versus three-round controlled bursts. The burst-control prevents ammunition wastage and is regarded as more accurate. There are situations in which full-auto is desirable, but these occur at close ranges and seldom are long bursts necessary. One instance in which it is desirable is the special forces practice in which a small team is engaged by a superior enemy force. To break contact the pointman empties his weapon in one full-automatic burst and rushes to the rear with the man behind him doing the same and so on until the enemy has had enough or the team outdistances them. Even without using this "banana peel" drill, it is common practice for a patrol's pointman to empty his weapon on full-auto when meeting the enemy.

While full-automatic (referred to as "rock 'n' roll" in Vietnam, but not as much as the movies would have you believe) may seem desirable, it is usually a waste of ammunition. The author tested this by firing five or six bursts from a 30-round magazine at a standard silhouette target at 50m. Only the first one or two rounds of each burst hit the target while the others zipped overhead. He next fired 30 rounds at another target in semi-automatic as fast as he could pull the trigger. The target was hit 28 times in a not much longer timespan than on full-automatic. The point is, it is hits that defeat the enemy, not who can make the most noise and clip the most tree limbs. Stoppages may also double with prolonged full-auto fire.

The integral carrying handle seemed like a good idea. Besides handily carrying the weapon, it served as a mount for the rear sight and protected it as well. Its rail had a hole in its center to mount a telescope or night vision sight. There were occasions when slingless rifles were attached to web gear by a snaplink through the carrying handle: for example, when being rope-extracted by helicopter or crossing rope bridges. A problem arose with prolonged rapid fire when heat transferred from the receiver to the carrying handle. This affected the rear sight and any attached telescope, and could burn the hand. Handle-carrying also reduced reaction time. It was preferred to carry the rifle at the ready at all times in the field. Some units prohibited carrying the weapon by the handle. With the

widespread introduction of the flat-top receiver in the late 1990s and the carrying handle's exclusion from issue in 2009 it has become a moot point.

In Vietnam replacement troops were typically issued a used M16 and a stack of magazines. This occurred when they were assigned to their division's replacement training center where they received minimal maintenance training. They usually had an opportunity to zero the weapon, but had little or no practice firing. This varied greatly by unit.

A Texas National Guardsman rappels down a Ft Hood, Texas cliff side with an M16A1 rifle slung cross-shoulder in the early 1970s. (Texas Military Forces Museum)

The author's own experience in 1969 was different. Benefiting from Special Forces weapons training and having more leeway than an infantryman, he was able to undertake more effective preparation than most troops were afforded. He was issued a new M16A1 and two cartons of seven 20-round magazines at the C-team (company HQ). At the B-team he drew ammunition and scrounged more magazines. He removed the sling swivels. On the forearm and butt he applied green duct tape to break up the black rifle's shape. At his A-team camp he was able to fire it for the first time, first disassembling it to clean and lubricate it by the book. He then fired 200 rounds at stumps and logs, anything man-sized, at different ranges. After cleaning it he zero-fired it followed by another 100 rounds, thoroughly cleaned it, and put in a new extractor spring. The magazines were cleaned and reloaded with 19 rounds with the third to the last a tracer to signal the magazine was near empty. Contrary to warnings, there is little chance of this alerting the enemy when numerous troops on both sides are firing.

The application of green tape to forearms and butts was common, but not widespread. The black rifle contrasts deeply in forests, deserts, and mountains. Black is not a naturally occurring color. In the 2000s some units spray-painted rifles for camouflage. In April 2010 the Tank-Automotive and Armaments Command (TACOM) issued permission to camouflage-paint M16/M4s if given command approval.

The author's M16A1 failed only once in combat. After several days of monsoon rains, during an engagement he was unable to move the selector lever from Safe. He ejected the magazine and used it to hammer the lever to Semi-auto. After the shootout, with a few drops of LSA and switching it back and forth it worked fine. Of the weapons belonging to the 400-man camp strike force, in a year the author made only four repairs on M16A1s – he fixed one broken extractor, one broken extractor spring, and two broken firing pins. In the field he carried a single spare firing pin in case one broke in his company. Less important repairs saw a few handguards being replaced. These were commonly broken, especially the right side; falling to the left generally protected the rifle, but protection was less if it fell to the right. So many right handguards were broken that there were often shortages.

In all post-Vietnam conflicts troops have arrived in-theater with their issue weapons, since now units rotate rather than individuals as in Vietnam. Active Army troops fire for qualification twice a year (National Guard and Reserves once) and conduct various live-fire and other exercises. Pre-deployment live-fire training is extensive and weapons are frequently re-zeroed in the theater of operations.

A French commando of the Bayonne-based 1st Marine Infantry Parachute Regiment (*1er Régiment de Parachutistes d'Infanterie de Marine – 1er RPIMa*), 2001. He is armed with an M4 carbine mounting an M203A1 grenade launcher. Note the weapon has been camouflage-painted, an increasingly common practice. However, certain components should not be painted: barrels (paint burns off), sights (can hamper adjustments), and magazines (prevents proper seating). (Jose Nicolas/Sygma/Corbis)

A former member of the 1st Infantry Division in Vietnam reported that when they exchanged M14s for XM16E1s there were only a half-dozen cleaning kits in the company. This made it difficult for over 100 men to clean their weapons. M14 cleaning gear could not be used. A few weeks later they received another two dozen kits to provide two or three per squad. Rifles frequently jammed on operations, sometimes after only a magazine or two. The cause was usually a sheared case in the chamber. A cleaning rod had to be passed to the soldier, who had to open the receiver, pull out the bolt carrier and operating handle, and punch the case out with the rod. In one firefight a man lost his operating handle in a rice paddy. In another firefight there were so many malfunctions that men were withdrawing. If it had not been for the two M60s the platoon would have been routed.

In firebases they had 20gal oil drums cut in half lengthwise and set on stands made from welded barbed-wire pickets. These were filled with gasoline or JP-4, and the rifles were broken down and scrubbed. A fire extinguisher was nearby and a guard posted to keep away unwary men smoking. Some men experienced easily infected hand and arm rashes because of this method. At first they had only 7.62mm cleaning patches and some men jammed them in M16 barrels because they didn't cut them in quarters.

A member of the 4th Infantry Division reported experiencing a broken extractor. He recovered a casualty's rifle and upon firing it noticed harder recoil. He continued to use it until the firing pin broke. Returning to base with both rifles he found there were no replacement parts available. The armorer removed the extractor from the second rifle and replaced the one on the soldier's rifle. He also discovered that the second rifle's recoil buffer was frozen. The added firing stress had probably contributed to the broken firing pin.

A member of the III Corps MIKE Force reported that during a stand-down the battalion undertook practice firing at a local range. Firing his XM177E2 at a target, it fired only one shot and failed to eject the case or recock. The charging handle had to be pulled back to eject and reload each round. Stripping the weapon revealed that the Allen head screws securing the gas key to the bolt carrier were loose, preventing gas from venting into the carrier to cycle the bolt. Normally these screws were "staked" to prevent their loosening. It could not be determined why they had loosened. He was thankful that this was discovered on the range instead of in a firefight. He swapped the bolt carrier with another from an M16A1 and it functioned for the rest of his tour.

A US Army advisor assigned to an ARVN infantry battalion in 1963 was, along with other advisors, issued an M16. The ARVN unit, though, still had M2 carbines and M1 rifles. Being advisors their job was to advise and assist, not fight, so the US personnel were not too concerned about ammunition incompatibility. They had only a half-dozen magazines apiece, but they carried numerous cartons of spare 5.56mm ammunition. What they had not counted on was the black rifle's firing signature. While conducting a sweep in the Mekong Delta a Viet Cong Main Force unit attacked the battalion's flank. One of the advisors, a captain, rushed to the action and found himself in a fierce firefight. When he opened fire he began to draw an increasing amount of return fire, forcing him to reposition. Every time he opened fire the return fire intensified, making his positions untenable. He was soon drawing fire from several different directions before discovering that not only were the Viet Cong firing on his unique-sounding weapon, but so were the ARVN. He wisely disengaged and rearmed himself with an M2 carbine on subsequent operations.

A member of the 5th Marines reported that they were issued XM16E1s in April 1967 by simply turning in their M14s and being handed a black rifle and a half-dozen magazines. They received no maintenance training. There was adequate cleaning gear and they zeroed the rifles and test-fired them before undertaking operations. They liked the light weight, but complained of too few magazines. It was not long before they encountered serious jamming. They cleaned the weapons daily but still had problems. Inspection teams insisted that it was the Marines' fault for inadequate cleaning. The common belief among the troops was that the inspectors were looking to blame anything but the rifle. Five months after receiving the M16A1 they had all the magazines they wanted.

In an August 1967 *Popular Science* article, "How Good is Our New Vietnam Rifle?", Herbert O. Johansen quoted a Marine writing home to his parents: "Before we left Okinawa we were all issued new M16 rifles. Practically every one of our dead was found with his rifle torn apart next to him where he had been trying to fix it."

Johansen accompanied a congressional investigation team and talked to over a dozen combat veterans. There were instances when the above occurred, but, "Only one [vet] had had a jam. It happened on a windy day when sand blew into the extractor. He cleaned it out in less than a minute and was back in business. That minute could mean the difference between life and death." Johansen also reported a Viet Cong prisoner claiming, "What we fear the most is the B-52 and the new little black weapon."

As can be seen, there were conflicting reports on experiences with M16s. This has occurred in every conflict in which it has seen service. The

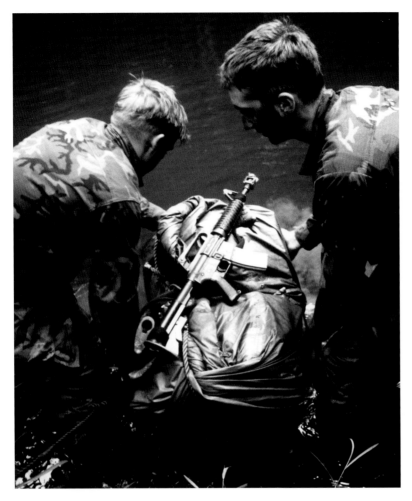

US Air Force Combat Control School students, training to be forward air controllers, launch an expedient poncho raft to float their rucksacks across a river at Pope Air Force Base, North Carolina, 1983. They are armed with GUU-5/P submachine guns, an upgrade of the earlier GAU-5-series with a birdcage suppressor rather than the old larger compensator. These are fitted with M15A1 blank adapters and 30-round magazines. (USAF)

M16A1 and M16A2 were used in the Gulf War and fine sand and dust proved to be an extreme problem. Besides issue muzzle covers, condoms were widely used. Excessive lubrication caused gumming problems and dry lubricants were not always effective. While the troops in Saudi Arabia had to struggle to keep their weapons clean leading up to the war, the ground war was short enough that few serious malfunctions occurred, especially since they had learned to care for them in the desert environment.

In Somalia, 1993, many soldiers reported that 6–10 hits were required to bring down a militant boosted by *khat*, an amphetamine-like stimulant. There is one claim that 40 rounds were required to bring down a drug-crazed gunman. Dust problems were also encountered in Mogadishu.

A 2006 survey by the Center for Naval Analysis found that 75 percent of soldiers reported overall satisfaction with the M16 and 88 percent with the M4. However, 19 percent reported that they had experienced a stoppage while in combat. Over 50 percent said they had experienced no stoppages with the M4 or M16A2/A4 in combat or during in-country training and practice firing. Rebuilt weapons (identified by an X after the serial number) were more likely to malfunction than those with original

parts. At the time 25 percent of troops were armed with the M4 and 49 percent with the M16 (other troops were armed with the M9 pistol or M249 SAW). The percentage of M4s has since increased.

Common recommendations included more robust magazines, higher magazine capacity, larger caliber or cartridges with more stopping power. M16 users were consistent and adamant about their desire to be issued M4s so as to have a more compact weapon. There were also complaints of M4s rapidly overheating and frequent parts breakage. At the battle for Wanat in July 2008, when a combat outpost was almost overrun, there were numerous complaints of the M4 being fired to excess in its three-round burst mode of 90–150rpm, the suppressive fire rate normal for M240 machine guns. This led to rapid overheating and parts breakage. One soldier burned out three M4s during the vicious fight.

Testing showed that exceeding the sustained rate of 15rpm meant that the weapon cooked off rounds in the chamber after some 170 rounds were fired. When the maximum rate of 90rpm was maintained for about 540 rounds the overheated barrel warped and gas escaped around the bullet. Further firing could actually cause the barrel to droop slightly and, after about 600 rounds, even burst.

In 2007 major extreme dust tests were conducted owing to continuing complaints from the field. The XM8 rifle, which had been canceled as a replacement for the M16/M4 in 2005, had 127 malfunctions out of 60,000 rounds, the FN Mk 16 Mod 0 had 226 malfunctions, the H&K HK416 had 233, and the M4 carbine had 882, resulting in a "significantly worse" rating.

Operation *Enduring Freedom*, 2008 (previous pages)

The US Marine Corps in Afghanistan and Iraq are armed with the M16A4 rifle and M4 carbine. Originally the M4 was not going to be used by the Marines, but it has been issued to all personnel previously armed with the 9mm M9 pistols, grenadiers, and others in infantry units. A great deal of latitude is allowed for the types and positioning of optical sights, night-vision devices, laser pointers, and attachments such as forward handgrips and bipods. The 40mm M203 grenade launcher seen here is mounted on the M4 carbine; it can also be mounted on the M16A4, but M4s tend to be used with grenade launchers owing to their lighter weight. The AN/PEQ-16 (the olive drab device fitted to the hand guard) is an LED white-light flashlight, infrared flood, infrared laser designator, and a visible laser. It has a two-week operational battery life. The Advanced Combat Optical Gunsight (ACOG) of various makes has become the standard sight for M16A4s and M4s. The carrying handles with rear sights are no longer issued with the M16A4. Used here are the Trijicon TA31 adopted by the Marines as the AN/PVQ-31A (for M16A4s) and AN/PVQ-31B (for M4s). These are 4×32 scopes replacing iron sights. A detachable backup iron sight is issued in case the ACOG is damaged. The M16A4-armed rifleman to the right has an AN/PEQ-2 laser-pointer mounted. It has two infrared laser emitters, one for aiming the rifle, and one wider beam for illuminating targets. The beams can only be seen through night-vision goggles, and this applies to the AN/PEQ-16. Many Marines carry a "dump pouch" as seen on the right hip of the leftmost man and the second man from the right. Empty magazines are dropped in this; it also provides stowage for a water bottle.

Soldier satisfaction (percent), Afghanistan/Iraq, 2006		
	M4	**M16A2/A4**
Weapon overall	88	75
Ammunition	79	79
Handling	90	60
Accuracy	94	89
Range	92	88
Rate of fire	93	88
Training	85	82
Maintainability	87	82
Cleaning equipment	75	68
Corrosion resistance	80	70
Accessories	86	75

5.56MM BULLET EFFECTS

It is true that while the 5.56mm could inflict terrible wounds, it also caused only minor wounds with direct hits and this led to another myth. It was said the M16 was designed *not* to kill, but only to wound. The "theory" was that a wounded soldier would require at least two men to take him off the battlefield and that this would overwhelm the enemy's medical services with wounded as well as affect morale. It is safe to say that morale is affected a lot more when troops are killed. Military doctrine has never been simply to wound the enemy, and a wounded enemy might still be able to fight back. Granted, there are instances when the enemy attempts to wound soldiers and use them as bait to fire on rescuers, but such incidents are simply taking advantage of the situation. Weapon developers do *not* design firearms with the aim of *only* wounding the enemy.

During the Vietnam War antiwar activists claimed that the 5.56mm M193 ball round was technically a "dum-dum bullet" because of its inherent yawing and tumbling effect when it strikes a person. This is totally incorrect. No law of war prohibits tumbling or unstable bullets. It cannot be prevented. To be a dum-dum the bullet has to be intentionally *modified* to cause more pain and suffering, for example by filing off the tip or drilling a hole into the core.

The various 5.56mm bullets have often been called "buzz-saw bullets" or the "meat ax" and claimed to tumble in flight or to tumble through human flesh once striking a person. The reality is different. Most small-caliber, high-velocity bullets are inherently unstable owing to the fact that the poorly balanced bullet is light in the nose and heavy in the base. Bullets really "want" to fly with the heavy end (the base) forward, but their spin-stabilized rotation keeps the point oriented forward. A bullet might yaw in flight, but it does not naturally tumble. Being unstable, so light a bullet traveling at a high velocity can easily be deflected by even small twigs. In this case the bullet will most likely tumble, be deflected to extreme angles, and not continue downrange on its intended trajectory. The bullet could break up as well. The same happens when the bullet penetrates light

The 5.56mm cartridge is now the standard caliber of squad-level weaponry. Four-man Marine fire teams have three M16A4 rifles, one mounting an M203 grenade launcher, and a 5.56mm M249 squad automatic weapon (SAW). Here, a fire team leader leads by example as his men rush forward during a training exercise at Camp Fuji, Okinawa. The M16A4s are fitted with M15A2 blank adapters. (US Navy)

materials such as sheetrock/drywall or plate glass, or exits a human body. The validity of the myth was enhanced when bullet holes were seen in cardboard targets that appeared to strike sideways. The assumption was that the bullet was tumbling before it hit the target. This was caused by the fact that the high-velocity bullet at a short range immediately went unstable when striking the target and "key-holed" – commenced to tumble – with the bullet apparently striking sideways.

When striking a human, the bullet becomes unstable in the same manner. Depending on the angle it strikes a body, its velocity at the instant of impact, and what combination of clothing, web gear, tissue, muscle, organs, voids, bone, etc it passes through, it may tumble half a turn, heavy end first. Going unstable on impact, the bullet may travel up to 4–5in in dense tissue and will attempt to orient itself heavy end first. It might make a 180-degree turn around its center of gravity, but that is all; it does not continue to tumble or "buzz saw." Additionally, the bullet is banded by a cannelure, a shallow groove around the bullet to which the cartridge case mouth is crimped. If striking bone it might break in two at the cannelure and some bits of the lead core and jacket might be expelled. This is especially possible at ranges under 100m owing to the high velocity. These dynamics are caused by physics and not by design. For 5.56mm weapons with a barrel under 14.5in long, like the XM177-series submachine gun and M4 carbine, this does not normally occur because of the lower velocity. This characteristic instability of lightweight high-velocity bullets is the cause of the 5.56mm round's main ballistic flaw, poor ability to penetrate typical materials used for cover. The following common barriers in urban areas stop a 5.56mm round fired at less than 50m: one layer of sandbags, one layer of bricks, a 2in unreinforced concrete wall, a 55gal sand or water-filled drum, a sand-filled small ammunition can, a sand-filled cinder block (the block may crack), or a plate glass windowpane at a 45-degree angle.

5.56mm M855 ball penetration, range 25–100m*

Initial represents rounds necessary to make a hole. *Loophole* represents rounds necessary to create an opening through which a weapon can be fired.

Material	Penetration	Rounds required
8in reinforced concrete	initial	35
"	loophole	250
14in triple brick and mortar	initial	90
"	loophole	160
12in concrete block with single brick veneer	loophole	60
"	breach hole	250
12in sand-filled cinder block	loophole	35
9in double brick wall	initial	70
"	loophole	120
24in double sandbag wall	initial	220
16in log wall	initial	1–3
0.375in mild steel door	initial	1

* *CALL Newsletter, Urban Combat Operations*, No. 99-16, November 1999

The twist ratio of the weapon's rifling has much to do with the bullet's stability and accuracy, as does the bullet's weight. M16 and M16A1 rifles, XM177-series submachine guns, and the M231 firing port weapon used the 5.56mm 55-grain M193 ball round and had a rifling twist of 1-in-12in. In 1980 the 62-grain M855 ball round was adopted by NATO. With a steel core it provides slightly better penetration, but it is only seven grains heavier than the M193 ball. This "heavier" bullet is more stable, with 1-in-9in rifling. To accommodate it the M16A2/A3/A4 rifles, M4 carbines, and M249 SAW are provided with a 1-in-7in twist. It is most effective for 40–60-grain bullets while 1-in-9in is best suited for 55–70-grain bullets, but the 1-in-7in twist was selected as a compromise to accommodate both

Members of the 6th Marines in Afghanistan, 2004. The Marine to the left is armed with an M16A4 rifle mounting an AN/PEQ-2 infrared illuminator on the right side and a white light flashlight beneath the handguard. The Marine to the right aims a SAM-R (Squad Advanced Marksman Rifle) similar to the Mk 12 Mod 0/1 Special Purpose Rifle (SPR) used by some special operations forces. This is a modified M16A4 allowing limited full-automatic fire (short bursts in emergency situations), fitted with a 20in match-grade barrel, mounting a TS-30A2 telescope (Leupold Mk 4 M3 3–9× illuminated riflescope), an AN/PEQ-2, improved iron sights, and a bipod. (USMC)

the new M855 ball and M856 tracer. There is an overlap in bullet applications. Some believe that one type of ammunition cannot be fired safely in the other's weapons. This is not true. Both types of rounds can be fired in any of the weapons. Accuracy will suffer, but only slightly and certainly not enough to affect combat firing at ranges under 100m.

The Viet Cong and North Vietnamese Army used captured M16A1 rifles and understood that these were lighter and fired faster (not always an advantage) than their AK-47/AKM. Regardless of all the accolades that proponents touted of the M16A1, the Viet Cong/North Vietnamese Army much preferred the more rugged and reliable AK-47/AKM and its better penetration. They conducted firing demonstrations to show this to their troops.

The extremes of M16 bullets' hits were seen by the author. A member of the author's A-team was hit by a Viet Cong-wielded M16A1 in the upper right arm at short range. The bullet went through the muscle without striking a bone. It was a clean wound resulting in little tissue damage. The soldier was back to duty in less than a week. On another occasion a North Vietnamese Army soldier was killed by multiple hits at short range. There were at least three killing wounds in the chest, but another had hit the back of the wrist, traveled up the length of the arm completely ripping it open to the bone, gone through the lower end of the upper arm just above the elbow, and took off the lower arm. It probably began to tumble after impact, resulting in a horrendous wound.

AMMUNITION CARRIAGE

The standard Army M16 basic load was nine 20-round magazines (180 rounds); only five 20-round magazines were carried for the M14. Fortunately, four M16 magazines could be carried in the M1956 magazine pouch designed to carry two M14 magazines. The pouch was too deep, though, and often a field dressing was placed in the bottom to raise the M16 magazines. In Vietnam, soldiers carried anywhere from 13 to over 20 magazines. There were shortages of pouches and often they carried one or two seven-pocket bandoliers, placing a magazine in each pocket. In 1968 a shortened version of the M14-type pouch was provided for M16s, soon followed by the M1967 nylon pouch. Special reconnaissance teams often carried five magazines in 1-quart canteen carriers, while others used M1937 BAR belts with six four-M16-magazine pockets, although other items were carried in some pockets.

The first Marine units receiving M16s were often only issued three magazines; this was totally inadequate for a semi-automatic, let alone an automatic weapon. The rest of their ammunition was issued in 20-round cartons. The seven-pocket bandoliers containing ten-round stripper clips, enabling magazines to be reloaded rapidly, were not available until well into 1967. They had to reload their three magazines one round at a time. The Marines used the M1963 pouch; this held one M14 magazine and could not be used for M16 magazines. They mostly used bandoliers to

carry magazines, placed them in the large pockets on the M1953 armor vest, or acquired some Army M1956 pouches. Soon, 5.56mm was issued tactically in 140-round M3 bandoliers (14× 10-round stripper clips) with six bandoliers in an 840-round metal can and two cans per wooden box.

With the advent of the 30-round magazine in the early 1970s, new magazine carriers were necessary. The All-purpose Lightweight Individual Carrying Equipment (ALICE) gear was fielded in 1975, although the new pouches were issued in late 1974. These held three 30-round magazines and two were issued per man with seven magazines (210 rounds). ALICE was replaced by the Individual Tactical Load Bearing Vest (ITLBV) or Individual Integrated Fighting System (IIFS) in 1988. This system provided four two-magazine and two one-magazine pockets. The Marines used the ALICE and ITLBV as well. The seven-pocket bandolier was replaced by a four-pocket one with each pocket holding three ten-round clips (for 120 rounds).

Next was the Modular Lightweight Load-carrying Equipment (MOLLE – pronounced "Molly"), which saw wide distribution by 2001. It allowed varied configurations tailored to a soldier's needs. The standard rifleman's configuration is three two-magazine pouches and two three-pocket side-by-side pouches for 12 magazines. More pouches can be added and the canteen/general-purpose pouch can hold five magazines. The Marines used MOLLE until fielding the Improved Load Bearing Equipment (ILBE) in 2005 with three two-magazine pouches and a

Members of the 36th Infantry Division in Iraq. They are armed with M16A4 rifles, M4 carbines, and M203 grenade launchers. All mount ECOS-N M68 close-combat optical sights. They carry MOLLE web gear. In the background is an up-armored HMMWV. (Texas Military Forces Museum)

speed/reload pouch; more pouches can be added. Pouches can also be attached to the Marines' Modular Tactical Vest (MTV) with no need for the ILBE vest. Some servicemen purchase "stock pouches" that strap on the butt's side holding a single backup magazine.

LAW-ENFORCEMENT USE

Many law-enforcement agencies – the FBI, CIA, Customs and Border Protection, and other Federal agencies, as well as many police and sheriff's departments and the Texas Rangers – use M16s, M4s, and CAR-15s, mostly purchased new, but also military surplus. This is a direct result of the increased use of AK-47s, M16s, and other "assault rifles" by criminal elements, especially since the 1990s.

This became painfully apparent during the North Hollywood, California, bank robbery attempt executed in February 1997 by two drugged gunmen wearing heavy body armor. They were armed with three AK-47-type rifles (modified to fire full-automatic), an HK41 semi-automatic rifle, a Bushmaster XM15 (automatic), and a 9mm pistol. They were spotted entering a bank by the Los Angeles Police Department, and a 44-minute shootout ensued. The dozens of responding police officers were armed only with 9mm and .38cal handguns and a single shotgun. Some were able to commandeer AR-15s from a gun store, but they were still outgunned, even after some M16-armed Special Weapons and Tactics (SWAT) officers arrived. The two fleeing robbers were killed after taking multiple hits, but 11 officers and seven civilians were wounded. The perpetrators fired 1,100 rounds and the police 650. The shootout resulted in a debate about providing police with additional firepower. There had been earlier incidents in which the police were outgunned, though not as extreme as the North

A SWAT team member unloads M4 carbines from his vehicle. This was in response to a 2007 shooting incident inside a shopping mall in Omaha, Nebraska, where nine people were killed including the gunman. Both M4s are fitted with reflex sights. (Chris VanKat/Reuters/Corbis)

Hollywood shootout. Six months later the Department of Defense provided 600 M16s to the Los Angeles Police Department and these were issued to patrol sergeants. Other police departments, large and small, followed suit by issuing M16s and M4s, both selective fire and semi-automatic only, and including many commercial variants.

Besides conventional armies and law enforcement, M16s and variants are widely used by paramilitary forces, militias, terrorists, crime gangs, and guerrillas the world over. Many of these unconventional forces prefer AK-47s, but the M16 is widely used owing to availability. A large number of those in use were pilfered, hijacked, obtained as spoils of war, or sold on the black market. Many of the M16s used by illicit organizations were obtained from military stocks of Latin American countries. This applies to the numerous M16s entering Mexico, not from the USA as is often claimed, but illegally transferred from Latin American countries. These weapons were originally acquired from the USA through Foreign Military Sales (government-to-government purchase) or through Foreign Military Financing grants given to foreign governments to purchase American-made weapons.

Police SWAT team members from Texas with a Colt M4 carbine and an M16A2 rifle. The carbine model has a slightly longer barrel than military M4s. These officers were dispatched to aid New Orleans in the aftermath of Hurricane Katrina, 2005. (C.J. Harper)

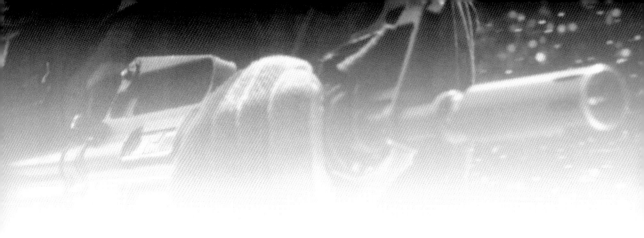

IMPACT
The iconic "toy" rifle

While probably the most controversial small arm to be adopted by the US armed forces and one of the more problem-plagued and criticized, the M16 is the most widely produced small arm to see US service. To date an estimated eight million of all variants have been produced and production continues. This includes licensed copies produced in Canada, Korea, Philippines, and Singapore, but not unlicensed knockoffs such as the Chinese CQ-556, Iranian DIO-S5.56, Filipino Armada, and Sudanese Terab. For comparison approximately 6,250,000 M1, M2, and other carbines have been produced followed by 4,040,000 M1 rifles and variants, and almost 1,400,000 M14 rifles and variants. The most prolific of modern weapons are the AK-series with an estimated 75 million assault rifle variants along with 25 million other variants (light machine guns, submachine guns etc).

The M16/M4 has become an icon of American culture; it has been the soldier's and Marine's primary individual weapon since the mid-1960s and will continue to be for the foreseeable future. The term "black rifle," referring to many modern assault weapons, originated with the M16. It has been used as a battle rifle, carbine, submachine gun, designated marksman rifle, match rifle, and infantry fighting vehicle defense weapon. During the Vietnam War it became symbolic, along with the M79 grenade launcher. The M16 is the most widely produced 5.56×45mm rifle in the world. It is in use by 15 NATO countries and over 80 other countries worldwide. Approximately 90 percent are estimated to remain in operation, although that figure might be somewhat high.

The M16/M4 is also widely used by law-enforcement agencies and is extremely popular among US civilian shooters, especially those involved in 5.56mm marksmanship and police-type assault weapon competitions. There are countless accessories, magazines, attachments, and after-market components available to drastically modify and upgrade personalized versions. This is so popular within certain circles that an obsession with AR-15/M16/M4s is known as BRD (black rifle disease). Paintball and Airsoft (plastic pellet-firing air rifle) replicas of M16/M4s are also produced. M16s have seen some use in small game and varmint hunting.

The terms "AR-15" and "M16" are considered generic. However, Colt maintained that it was the trademark holder for "M4," especially since the spread of BRD, with M4-like knockoffs being called an "M4gery" – a contraction of "M4" and "forgery." In December 2005 a Maine District Court judge ruled in favor of Bushmaster Firearms, dismissing Colt's claims of trademark infringement, and ruling that "M4" is a generic name, and that Colt's trademark should be revoked.

The often-maligned 5.56×45mm cartridge is now among the world's four most-used combat cartridges – along with the 7.62×51mm NATO for rifles and machine guns, the Soviet/Russian 7.62×39mm used in AK-series assault rifles, and the 9×19mm Parabellum used in submachine guns and pistols. The 5.56×45mm has been one of the standard NATO cartridges since 1980 and is in use by many other countries. The round has its limitations and faults, but it continues to be improved and developed.

Thousands have perished before the muzzle of the M16/M4, but perhaps its most notorious target was Osama bin Laden who may have met his double-tapped fate at the end of an HK416 (based on the M4A1) or a Colt 7.62mm CM901 carbine (an AR-10 spin-off) wielded by a SEAL.

A commercial Colt M4 carbine used by a Texas SWAT team fitted with a sound suppressor, a reflex sight, and add-on fore grip. This type of fore grip provided better control during full-automatic fire. (Ammunition in the foreground is .45 ACP.) (C.J. Harper)

REPLACEMENT

The two major complaints associated with the M16/M4 are its susceptibility to sand and dust and increased failures with exceedingly high and prolonged rates of fire. Virtually every conflict the US has been involved in since 1990 has taken place in a hot, often dry, dusty and sandy environment. There are also seasonal rains and cold weather in some of the areas. There is no reason to expect this to change. In the usually close-quarters combat situations of counterinsurgency conflicts, in which high sustained rates of fire are often demanded, weapons must be able to measure up to the task. The utopian idea of ultra-lightweight weapons of composite and synthetic materials is unrealistic. Other complaints center on the weapon's poor penetration, erratic effects on human targets, lack of range, and inaccuracy – usually attributed to the 5.56mm round, but aggravated by the M4's short barrel.

The Army countered the complaints surrounding the M4 by claiming that troops were generally satisfied with the weapon, but desired modifications. A number of replacements have been proposed and studied. During the Vietnam War the Marines considered the Stoner 63 system as an M16 replacement, but dropped it. The Army tested a series of .17cal (4.32mm) flechette-round-firing rifles in the Special Purpose Individual Weapon (SPIW) Program from the 1960s into the 1970s. The program failed because of poor penetration and the inability to provide armor-piercing and tracer rounds. Caseless ammunition was also tested in this period.

The Advanced Combat Rifle (ACR) Program commenced in 1986, testing the AAI Corporation flechette rifle, H&K G11 using caseless ammunition, Steyr flechette-firing rifle, Eugene Stoner's Ares Inc. Advanced Individual Weapon System, and the Colt M16A2E2. The program was dropped as the more futuristic weapons demonstrated too many problems needing prolonged development or were not a significant improvement over existing weapons.

The Objective Individual Combat Weapon (OICW) Program began in the late 1990s, resulting in two H&K-developed potential replacements. The first was the XM29, a 5.56mm assault weapon mounting an integral 20mm "smart" semi-automatic grenade launcher. Far too heavy, complex, and expensive, it was canceled in 2004. The next OICW offering was the 5.56mm XM8 rifle, carbine, compact carbine, and automatic rifle. On the verge of adoption, it was canceled in 2005 as it was not sufficiently advanced over the M16/M4 and M249 SAW. It was proven better in a sandy/dusty environment than the M4.

A very popular contender is the 5.56mm HK416 (its designation derived from "M4/M16"), which uses the M4A1 lower receiver and has a "drop-in" upper receiver and barrel. It also requires a new buffer. Its short-stroke piston and operating rod replace the M4A1's direct impingement system. Introduced by H&K in 2005 and adopted by Delta Force, SEALs, and other special units, the HK416 may be the wave of the future, allowing existing lower receivers to be retained, with the much-improved upper and barrel incorporating 90 percent of the upgrades.

Israeli soldiers in the Gaza Strip, 1993. Both are armed with M4 carbines. The soldier in the foreground has a baton launcher fitted. This fires a 40mm "rubber bullet," actually a semi-soft or hard plastic round-nose projectile muzzle-loaded into the launcher and propelled by a special launcher round. Considered a "less than lethal" riot control munition, they have caused occasional deaths, especially with a head strike. (Peter Turnley/Corbis)

Other partial M4 replacements include the FN 5.56mm Mk 16 Mod 0 Light (SCAR-L) and the 7.62mm Mk 17 Mod 0 Heavy (SCAR-H) special forces combat assault rifles issued to some Ranger and SEAL units in 2009. Further purchases of the 5.56mm Mk 16 were halted in 2010, however, it not being a major improvement over the M4A1.

The Lightweight Small Arms Technologies (LSAT) Program began in 2008 and is a conceptional assault rifle concept. No prototypes exist as it is a study of new technologies, materials, and cased and caseless ammunition.

In January 2011 the Army invited manufacturers to submit candidates for the M4's replacement. (They had been alerted to this three years earlier.) The solicitation does not specify a specific caliber. While most offerings are 5.56mm (which has the most potential for winning owing to NATO ammunition and magazine standardization), others are 6.8mm SPC, 6.5mm Grendel, 7.62×51mm NATO, and 7.62×39mm (AK-caliber). The Remington Adaptive Combat Rifle, for example, allows the user to change from 5.56mm to 6.8mm by quickly changing the bolt head, barrel, and magazines. Others are also changeable.

Even though a new weapon may be adopted to replace the M4 (which would require several years of testing and development before even limited fielding), the Army is working on a product improvement program to upgrade the over 500,000 existing M4s, probably with a "drop-in" upper and barrel. Regardless of what weapon may be adopted as the M4's replacement, the M16A2/A3/A4 will remain in support units for many years, to say nothing of its continued use by other countries. The M16 has already been in US military service for 50 years. It is conceivable that it will be on the battlefield for at least another 20.

GLOSSARY

BALL: Standard full-metal-jacketed bullet

BOLT CARRIER: An assembly containing the bolt to perform chambering, firing (via firing pin) and ejection, and the gas key interlinking the assembly and the gas tube

BUFFER: A tubular assembly contained in the M16/M4's butt to reduce recoil; officially the "recoil spring guide"

CARTRIDGE DEFLECTOR: A lip to the rear of the ejection port on M16/M4 receivers preventing ejected cases from striking the face of left-handed firers

CLOSED BOLT OPERATION: A weapon that fires the first round with the bolt closed (locked). After each shot the bolt remains forward

COOK-OFF: When a chambered round in a very hot weapon is detonated by the heat. If the weapon is on full-automatic it will continue to fire until empty, a "runaway gun"

FLASH SUPPRESSOR: A muzzle device that helps reduce flash and recoil

FLAT-TOP RECEIVER: An M16/M4 upper receiver with a detachable carrying handle (with rear sight) that can be removed to attach optical sights

FORWARD ASSIST DEVICE (FAD): A plunger on the right side of most M16/M4 receivers that is struck by the palm of the hand after chambering a cartridge to ensure the bolt is locked

GAS TUBE: The thin tube through which propellant gas is vented to cause the weapon to operate by driving the bolt carrier back after each shot

Mk/MOD: Materials designated by Mark and Modification are Navy proponency while Army proponency items are designated by Model (M). Any service may use the others' materials

OPEN BOLT OPERATION: A bolt that is held in the open position (i.e. not closed to lock the breech) before firing. When the first shot is fired the bolt slams forward, chambering a round and firing it. When the last round is fired the bolt remains open and the chamber empty to aid in weapon cooling and preventing a "cook-off"

PICATINNY RAIL: MIL-STD-1913 "tactical rails" or "STANAG 2324 rails" are integral track-like brackets fitted on weapons for mounting sights, night vision devices, light sources, handgrips, and other accessories (pronounced "Pick uh TIN nee")

RECEIVER: The main body of the weapon containing the operating mechanism. The M16/M4 has an upper receiver with the bolt carrier and recoil buffer to which the barrel is attached, while the lower receiver has the firing mechanism, trigger, magazine housing, and butt stock

SPORTS: Slap, Pull, Observe, Release, Tap, and Shoot. The sequence of the immediate action drill to correct a malfunctioning M16/M4

STRIPPER CLIP: Ten-round charging clips for loading cartridges into magazines

YAWING: The bullet wobbling in flight as opposed to tumbling end over end

SELECT BIBLIOGRAPHY

Secondary sources

Bartocci, Christopher R. *Black Rifle II: The M16 into the 21st Century*. Cobourg, Canada: Collector Grade Publications, 2004

Ezell, Edward C. *The Great Rifle Controversy: Search for the Ultimate Infantry Weapon from World War II Through Vietnam and Beyond*. Harrisburg, PA: Stackpole Books, 1984

Green, Michael and Stewart, Greg. *Weapons of the Marines*. St. Paul, MN: Motorbooks International, 2004

Huon, Jean. *The M16*. Havertown, PA: Casemate, 2004

Poyer, Joe. *The M16/AR15 Rifle: A Shooter's and Collector's Guide*. Tustin, CA: North Cape Publications, 2003

Stevens, R. Blake, Blake, R., and Ezell, Edward C. *The Black Rifle: M16 Retrospective*. Toronto, Canada: Collector Grade Publications, 1987

Military manuals

DA Pam 750-30 *The M16A1 Rifle Operation and Preventive Maintenance*. July 1969 (also June 1968). (Department of the Army Pamphlet) Available online: <http://www.ep.tc/problems/25/index.html>

FM 3-22.9 *Rifle Marksmanship: M16A1, M16A2/3, M16A4 and M4 Carbine*. April 2003. (Field Manual) Available online: <http://www.globalsecurity.org/military/library/policy/army/fm/3-22-9/index.html>

FM 23-9 *M16A1 Rifle and Rifle Marksmanship*. June 1974

FM 23-9 *Rifle, 5.56mm, M16A1*. March 1970

FM 23-9 *Rifle, 5.56mm, XM16E1*. July 1966

FMFM 0-9 *Field Firing for the M16A2 Rifle*. June 1995. (Fleet Marine Force Manual)

TM 9-1005-319-10 *Operator's Manual for Rifle, 5.56mm, M16A2, M16A3, and M16A4, and Carbine, 5.56mm, M4 and M4A1*. June 2010. (Technical Manual) Available online: <http://www.coschooloffirearms.com/10levelm16m4.pdf>

INDEX